Understanding Leadership

formerly

What makes a Leader?

John Eddison

SCRIPTURE UNION

47 MARYLEBONE LANE, LONDON, W1M 6AX

By the same author

Understanding the Ten Commandments
Understanding Ourselves
Understanding Basic Beliefs
It's a Great Life
Christian Answers about Doctrine
Who Died Why

© John Eddison 1974
First published 1974
ISBN 0 85421 4550

Printed in Great Britain
by Unwin Brothers Limited
The Gresham Press
Old Woking
Surrey

A member of the Staples Printing Group

To E. J. H. N.

with affection and respect

Note from the Author

Every Christian preacher or writer runs the risk of being thought dogmatic—of laying down the law, and trying to get away with assertions which he would not be allowed to get away with in open debate. It is an occupational hazard—and one which preachers often correct to some extent by personal conversation or group discussion, which can have a very real value as a sequel to (though not as a substitute for) the original proclamation.

For writers it is more difficult, but this is why, at the end of each chapter in this book, I have included a number of questions. These are intended partly for further Bible study—and also as starting-points for useful group discussion. They give readers the chance to examine more closely what the chapter is saying, to apply it to the practical issues of daily life, and even to challenge some of the basic assumptions I have made.

It is suggested, for example, that the members of a group should study a chapter on their own, and then come together perhaps once a week to discuss it, each member of the group making himself responsible to lead the discussion of one particular question. It is hoped that in this way the book will, so to speak, assume another dimension, and prove of additional value to the reader.

JOHN EDDISON

Contents

Introduction

One of the most popular complaints today is that the country and indeed the world lacks leadership. On all sides the cry goes up, 'Where have all the leaders gone?' Where are the great reformers, orators and pioneers of a hundred years ago?

It is a question which, I must confess, I do not find myself asking. I think it is the habit of each generation to look back on the past and to say that 'there were giants in the earth in those days', but I don't think it was so. The leaders of the past always appear larger than life, and no doubt Victorians regarded Disraeli and Gladstone in much the same way as we regard Heath and Wilson today.

But there is of course one big difference, and that is that the leaders of the past were never exposed as they would be today to the intense publicity of the mass media—press, radio and television. It is almost impossible, for example, for a man or woman to stand up to the battering of television interviews and retain an impression of greatness. He is cut down to size, and robbed of that aura which is supposed, perhaps quite falsely, to have surrounded his predecessors.

Again, we must be clear what we mean by a leader. It is easy to judge everyone by those men of genius who appear perhaps once in a generation. Very rarely do men as charismatic as Winston Churchill, William Temple, John F. Kennedy or Charles de Gaulle appear on the scene, and it is hardly fair to argue from the absence of such men today that there is a shortage of leaders. In fact it is probably true to say that there are as many ordinary run-of-the-mill leaders in church and politics, industry and the armed forces as there ever have been.

We must remember, too, that leadership nowadays is far more widely spread than in the past. There are those who set fashions in dress or life-style. There are those who command a large and devoted following in the press, or on radio or television. Such people can fairly claim to be called leaders, because thousands look up to them, believe what they say and accept them as their pattern.

Another factor to be borne in mind today is that the whole idea of leadership is out of favour. We are all encouraged to challenge authority, and to follow our own ideas and tastes.

To put it another way, people nowadays are much more difficult to lead, and take far less kindly than they used to do to the idea of leadership. They want to be allowed to do their own thing, and perhaps there is also a lurking fear of anything that savours of the Fuehrer-Prinzip which brought such disaster to Germany and Italy. We see the same thing in international relationships, for nationalism is simply individualism writ large; and the emerging countries want their independence. Colonialism is dead; paternalism is dying; and they would rather have freedom, even if it means making horrifying mistakes, than the old colonial security.

All this means that the task of leaders today is very much harder than it used to be. The result is that there are probably a good many people who prefer a comfortable life in an armchair to the controversial one in the hot seat which leadership in almost any field is likely to involve; and who can blame them. I have talked with boys, for example, who detest the idea of accepting responsibility, and with schoolmasters who cannot persuade those who might reasonably be expected to do so to occupy positions of authority.

One dangerous result of this attitude can be that the wrong sort of people get to the top—the seekers of power for its own sake; while others, taking the line of least resistance, find themselves outmanoeuvred and exploited. Nowhere has this effect been more clearly seen in recent years than in the Trades Union Congress.

Happily there are still those who are prepared to accept the challenge of leadership, to face unpopularity with those who do not want to be led at all or who want to be led in a different direction, and to spend their lives under the glaring spotlights of public scrutiny and criticism.

This book is intended to be a study of leadership as it was exercised by ten of the most outstanding people in the Bible. What are the qualities of leadership and, above all, what makes someone a spiritual leader—the sort of person who stands upon the Godward side of man and points men to Him? That is the question we shall be seeking to answer.

By studying these people, their weaknesses as well as their strengths, we may not arrive at any magic formula or recipe for successful leadership; but we shall I hope begin to appreciate some of those gifts and attributes, natural as well as moral and spiritual, which qualify men and women for positions of great responsibility.

1. Joseph—The Prime Minister

'From Durham Gaol to Downing Street.' That is how one of our popular newspapers might have introduced the memoirs of Joseph, had he lived in Britain in the twentieth century A.D. rather than in Egypt in the seventeenth century B.C., for it describes a leap which he made with hardly any intermediate steps, almost overnight.

In fact, his promotion was even more staggering than that because he was not only a prisoner, but an exile and a slave. He is the first example we have of the astonishing capacity of the Hebrews to get to the top. Daniel is another, but even Daniel, as we shall see, did not start with quite such handicaps as those which beset Joseph.

The story of Joseph's early life is quickly told. He and his youngest brother Benjamin were the sons of Rachel—Jacob's one true love. The other eight brothers were born to Leah (Rachel's bleary-eyed sister) and Bilhah and Zilpah (two household servants). It followed that Joseph and later Benjamin were the apple of their father's eye. Joseph could do little wrong and his father favoured him in a tactless and provocative way. Joseph used his privileged position to spy on his brothers and report their misdeeds to his father, and when we add to this the fact that he was both more talented than they and very conceited, we have all the ingredients for a first-class family row; and of course that is what happened.

Such envy and hatred did he inspire that when he came to visit his brothers, they determined to kill him and abandon him in a desert pit, where he would have died of thirst and exposure. However, there was a last-minute reprieve because a passing band of merchants gave his brothers the idea of profiting by his removal, and instead of leaving him to perish they sold him for twenty pieces of silver.

Once again his great good fortune held, for in Egypt, where he was taken by the Arabs, he became the possession of Pharaoh's Chief of Staff, a man named Potiphar, to whom he quickly made himself indispensable through his reliability and good sense. Everything seemed set fair until he fell foul of Potiphar's wife who, having failed to seduce him, accused him of trying to seduce her.

The next few years were spent in prison, and he might have languished there indefinitely if his ability to interpret dreams had not come to the ears of Pharaoh. He predicted a period of great prosperity, to be followed by one of scarcity, and Pharaoh was so impressed with his wisdom that he gave him almost unlimited powers, and Joseph became the second most important man in the kingdom. When the time came, the way he exercised these powers won universal approval, and when the lean years hit the whole of the Middle East, thanks to his foresight and prudence, Egypt found herself in a position of economic impregnability.

Such is the bare outline of the story, but it tells us little of the extraordinary qualities of the man himself. What incredible chain of circumstances led Egypt, surely for the first and last time in its history, to accept a Hebrew as Prime Minister? What turned a rather soft, spoilt and precocious child into one of the most benevolent autocrats of history?

I have had several times to act as a member of a selection committee for the appointment, for example, of a headmaster to a school. Without our always realizing it, there are, I think three things for which we are looking at every interview. Is the candidate equipped for the task by nature, by character and by experience? These are, so to speak, the three main tributaries of leadership.

It is tragic when we see a thoroughly good person 'hi-jacked' into a position of leadership for which *nature* never equipped him. It happened sometimes in the war, when a man who had handled a division competently enough had greatness thrust upon him and found that he had not got what it takes to command an army; and it happens from time to time in other walks of life as well.

Sometimes the mistake is seen in time and the man is allowed to find his way back again to his own level. Sometimes he is not so lucky and the parting of the ways comes only after a nervous breakdown or a major and disastrous mistake.

The responsibility for this sort of thing lies very much with those who make the selection, or encourage the man's application, perhaps by writing references which are misleadingly favourable. It is fair to no one to make out that the geese are swans, and a sober assessment of others is almost as important as a sober assessment of oneself. It should be obvious that God has not equipped all men and women to be leaders, nor to lead in the same kind of way.

But what are the natural gifts to look for in a would-be leader? What equips men and women for exalted and often lonely positions? There are too many exceptions to make it safe to look for any infallible rule, but there are certain qualities which never come amiss, and which are therefore worth considering in some detail.

To begin with, what about physical appearance? Does it count for anything? It can do so, but it is very danger-ous if taken on its own and not reinforced by deeper qualities. Absalom, for example, was exceptionally handsome, but his appearance was deceptive; and Paul, according to tradition, was not impressive to look at. Many other things have to be equal before much weight is given to a man's personal appearance, but if they are, it is a point in his favour. We are told nothing about

3

Joseph's looks, but the immediate impression he created upon people seems to have been favourable and authoritative and we can assume perhaps that 'he looked the part'. But we must be careful not to press this, and to remember that some of the great leaders of history have been physically insignificant and suffered perhaps from a squint or a stammer. Winston Churchill once said that some of the people who had influenced him most had been those who had impressed him least, that is by their physical presence. I have so often found that to be true in my own experience, that it has made me cautious of first and perhaps superficial impressions.

Then what about disposition? We need to know whether a man is temperamentally suited for his task. Will he crack under pressure? Will he flap if things go wrong? Can he keep his head when all about him are losing theirs? Is he prepared if necessary to be cordially disliked; for sometimes unpopularity goes with the job?

There is no doubt that Joseph was marvellously equipped in this respect. He faced many crises, personal, domestic, national, and came through them all. The names he gave his two sons reflect his own strong temperament, for Manasseh means 'forgetful' and Ephraim 'fruitful'. In other words it was as though he said to himself, 'I am not going to allow myself to be haunted by the past or daunted by the future'.

The next thing that we notice about Joseph is that he was a man of very sound judgement. We see this in the conspicuously successful way in which he handled the economic crisis, and the universal applause which his policies earned. Pharaoh never had reason to alter his first impression: 'There is no one so shrewd and intelligent as you . . . I hereby give you authority over the whole land of Egypt' (Genesis 41: 39, 40).

It goes without saying too that he was by nature industrious and not afraid of hard work. He was the kind of man who could be left to find his way to the heart of a problem and rapidly sort it out; who could rally the loyalty of subordinates and communicate his decisions intelligently to others.

And Joseph had imagination. There are hints of this in the dreams he had as a boy. 'Some people see things as they are and ask "Why?",' said Robert Kennedy. 'I like to see things as they might be and to say "Why not?".' It is this sort of imaginative approach that is needed so much today—the attitude of mind that sees visions, that takes risks, that makes experiments. In my experience as a governor of many schools, I have always found that one secret of progress is for the Head to be the accelerator, having the ideas and seeing the visions, and for the governors to apply the brakes of financial caution and control. To have it the other way round will always breed delay and stagnation.

Joseph, too, was a first class administrator. You sometimes hear people speaking disparagingly of administration as though it were of little importance, and compared unfavourably with more 'spiritual' gifts; but it is the framework within which all leadership is exercised; and a would-be leader can only ignore this gift at his peril.

Certainly it is clear that Joseph possessed it and was a born organizer. He must have known how to fit others into his team, how to make them work together and how to get the best out of them. We can imagine that letters were answered at once, engagements punctually kept, complaints carefully examined and problems sifted and sorted out.

It is true that most leaders can pick their staff and delegate much of the administration; but the leader himself must be prepared to do his own homework, to learn his job and to organize his time. Have you not often found that if you want something efficiently done it pays to give it to the busiest person you can find because you know that he will be so well disciplined that he will be sure to find a time-slot into which he can fit you and your particular problem?

When we turn to Joseph's *character*, the thing which strikes us most is his integrity. His first boss, Potiphar, quickly discovered this and we are told that 'He left everything he possessed in Joseph's care, and concerned himself with nothing but the food he ate' (Genesis 39: 6). How many others have tried to do the same and have been hopelessly let down and made to look foolish and gullible! But Potiphar knew his man. He knew he could trust Joseph with everything he possessed, even his wife. Indeed it has been suggested that Potiphar never accepted his wife's story, for had he really believed Joseph to be guilty of adultery, death and not prison would have been the punishment.

The next man to make this discovery was the governor of the prison, for we are told that 'He put Joseph in charge of all the prisoners in the tower and of all their work. He ceased to concern himself with anything entrusted to Joseph' (Genesis 39: 22, 23). What a remarkable tribute! It shows that Joseph's reputation must have preceded him, and fancy his being able to hold such a position without losing the confidence and respect of his fellow prisoners!

Then it was Pharaoh's turn to discover what an extraordinary young man had entered his kingdom. For after he had interpreted Pharaoh's dreams and been promoted to the rank of Prime Minister, Pharaoh said to him, 'You shall be in charge of my household and all my people will depend on your every word' (Genesis 41: 40). Joseph, in other words, was a man he knew he could trust implicitly.

And surely this is what people always want of their leaders, whether political, military or ecclesiastical. They are suspicious of the very clever, they mistrust the very charming and they dislike the ambitious; but if they know a man is transparently honest in his personal and official life, they are more than content.

'Integrity' is an interesting word. It means 'wholeness' or 'untouchedness', and an 'integer' is a 'whole or intact or undivided number'. What gives a man this undivided quality? Nothing more effectively than a single-minded devotion to God. This brings together the different and even perhaps conflicting parts of his personality—reason, conscience, emotion and will, harmonising them into one main purpose so that in the truest sense the man himself becomes integrated. Wherever you tap his life, there is the ring of truth about it.

This is how it was with Joseph. It was his loyalty to God that drew together all his faculties and provided him with his magnetic north; or to change the metaphor, his faith was the string on which were threaded all the various beads of personality and experience.

It was this faith, too, which upheld him in the dark days in prison and which kept him humble in the palace. We have talked of good fortune and luck, but it is doubtful whether Joseph would have approved of such language; for when at the end of his story he accepted his brothers' apology, he said, 'You thought evil against me; but God meant it unto good' (Genesis 50: 20). Like Browning he could say, 'Let one more attest; I have lived, seen God's hand through a lifetime and all was for best.'

And it was his faith, too, which left him unembittered and magnanimous towards those who had wronged him. One of the marks of a great man is whether he can exercise authority without becoming arrogant or vindictive. Joseph passed that test. His treatment of his brothers may at first seem a little strange, but we must remember that he had to teach them a lesson. He had to assure himself that they were truly penitent and that they would not desert Benjamin as they had deserted him. But once he knew that their sorrow was the kind that leads to repentance, we are told that 'he could no longer control his feelings' (Genesis 45: 1).

'So loudly did he weep that the Egyptians and Pharaoh's household heard him' (Genesis 45: 2). Some people think that tears are a sign of weakness. Not so. Jesus wept, and there is surely something the matter with a man or woman who is so 'uptight' that he is incapable or ashamed of tears. There are some things that can only be said with tears: 'If you have tears, prepare to shed them now.'

But Joseph was not only endowed by nature and character. He was also equipped by *experience* for the tremendous responsibilities he was destined to carry.

At seventeen, as we have seen, he was the pampered favourite of his father, by that time a widower. There is no doubt, too, that he exploited his privileged position and behaved in a tactless and conceited way towards his half-brothers. He really got the sort of treatment which, by the standards of those days, he deserved.

Then calamity fell, but with it came the training and experience he so badly needed. It took two forms. He met with triumph and disaster. He was taught to face success without undue elation and failure without dismay. In Potiphar's household he got his first taste of independent responsibility. Coping with domestic affairs, he prepared himself for dealing with men and money on a national scale.

The time in prison must have seemed endless, but here again God was with him, and in one translation of Psalm 105: 18 we are told that 'The iron entered into his soul.' What had been soft and pliable became firm and strong as tempered steel, so that when the final test came, he was able to stand up to Pharaoh and to steer the country through what could have been a catastrophic economic crisis.

There is a sense, as Tennyson says, in which 'I am part of all that I have met,' and the mistakes and lessons of the past can be woven into the fabric of our personalities and used to clothe and equip us for the future. For what after all is knowledge except, as Carlyle reminds us, 'recorded experience'?

But of course not everyone learns by experience. Sometimes it is a harsh unwelcome teacher and we shrink from and evade its lessons. Joseph was different. The tactlessness gave way to shrewdness and diplomacy, the softness to strength, the conceit to humility.

Again and again I have come across cases of people whose influence for good has been enriched by what they have suffered. I remember a well-known Christian speaking gratefully about Psalm 16: 6—'The lines are fallen unto me in pleasant places; yea, I have a goodly heritage.' He was applying them to himself, and the affluent life he enjoyed. Soon afterwards I heard that he had passed through a very severe financial crisis, but he came through it triumphantly, and his witness for Christ was all the more effective because of what he had suffered. I can think of an over-busy parson who had become, perhaps, a little too professional, and was hit by a long and incapacitating illness. Instead of blaming God and resenting this experience, he allowed it to bring a new depth and strength into his ministry. I know a man who has experienced a series of bitter disappointments in his career, but who bears no grudge, and whose life is mellowed by what he has been through.

And so I could go on. In fact I wonder whether anyone can exercise really effective leadership unless, like Paul, he has suffered, and known the meaning of a 'thorn in the flesh' (2 Corinthians 12: 7). This is partly because it is so often the case that character is forged in the fires of affliction; and partly because only those who have suffered can be truly sympathetic with others and sensitive to their problems.

W. E. Sangster tells the story of a man who wanted to illustrate this to a friend. It was in the comparatively early days of the gramophone record, and he played the same piece twice, and asked his friend which rendering he preferred. 'The second,' said the friend, 'it was altogether better. But why?' 'The first time I used a steel needle,' was the reply, 'but on the second occasion I played it with a thorn.'

Nature, character, experience—these were the foundations on which the leadership of this remarkable man was built. It is not given to many to rise as he did to become to such an extent a man of destiny; but for every Christian 'There is a divinity that shapes his ends, rough-hew them how he will.'

Discussion Points

1. Joseph has been called 'the most Christ-like man in the Old Testament'. In what ways do his character and experience remind you of Jesus? (Compare, for example, Matthew 3: 17, John 1: 12, Matthew 26: 14, 15, 1 Peter 2: 19–23, Acts 4: 10–12.)
2. To what extent was Joseph's life an illustration of the truth expressed in Romans 8: 28?
3. Which of Joseph's qualities do you think is most lacking in the leadership of this country today in (a) politics, and (b) the Christian Church?
4. How far should a Christian try to cultivate the gift of being a good administrator? How can we do this?
5. What can a 'rising star' like Joseph do to stop his colleagues envying him?
6. Should we always forgive unconditionally those who have wronged us? Or should we sometimes say, 'I will forgive you, if . . .'?

2. Moses—The Chief Justice

Moses has always been a focus of attention for men and women who have aspired to great office. Field-Marshal Montgomery described him as the greatest leader of all time; and Sir Winston Churchill devotes a complete chapter to him in his book *Thoughts and Adventures*. Indeed, his summary of Moses' remarkable career can hardly be improved upon: 'he was the greatest of the prophets who spoke in person to the God of Israel; he was the national hero who led the chosen people out of the land of bondage through the perils of the wilderness and brought them to the very threshold of the promised land; he was the supreme lawgiver who received from God that remarkable code upon which the religious, moral and social life of the nation was so· securely founded. Tradition lastly ascribed to him the authorship of the pentateuch, and the mystery that surrounded his death added to his prestige.'

Moses is perhaps the outstanding example of the maxim that 'God matches His moments with His men.' Consider the situation. Under Joseph's enlightened Pharaoh, the Hebrews had been hospitably received into Egypt and given their own territory on the north-east frontier which was known as the land of Goshen. Here they multiplied exceedingly, and from being a welcome group of strangers they had become a political and social problem. The result was that a wave of anti-Semitism, so common in our day, had swept through the country and 'the children of Israel were reduced by the policy of the state and the prejudices of its citizens, from guests to servants and from servants almost to slaves'.

The policy took two forms: exploitation and suppression. They provided cheap labour for Pharaoh to build his great treasure cities of Pythom and Rameses, which were the granaries of the Middle East in those days, and as important as the oil-producing countries of today. So in this respect the Hebrews were a national asset and were exploited to the full. On the other hand, there was the fear that they would become too numerous and therefore a threat to the security of the kingdom, and so Pharaoh ordered that most brutal form of birth control, namely infanticide, in an attempt to arrest the increase of male Israelites.

It was at this point that Moses was born. For some time he was successfully concealed in his own home, but when that proved to be no longer possible a clever strategy was devised whereby, as a seemingly abandoned baby, he should be allowed to attract the attention of Pharaoh's daughter.

If the plan succeeded and the Princess had compassion on the infant boy, then there was every hope that he would be brought up in her household, nursed by his own mother who was standing by to offer her services as soon as he was discovered on the river bank. It was a daring plan, but the child's only hope of survival, and it worked; and it is here perhaps that we can first detect the sign of God's providential hand.

If it was in God's mind to use Moses as the great liberator of His chosen people, then clearly his background and upbringing were of great importance. He must be unmistakably a Hebrew, one of his own people identified with them both in their sufferings and their aspirations. At the same time, he must be able to stand up to Pharaoh and to put the case of his people with an authority and skill which he could only acquire as an

Egyptian. He must in other words be an Egyptian-Hebrew.

We see the same sort of divine care in the way in which God prepared Saul of Tarsus. He described himself as a Hebrew of the Hebrews and yet he could claim Roman citizenship. We see perhaps the supreme example of the same principle at work in Jesus Himself, who was both human and divine, Son of Man and Son of God.

This sort of 'dual personality' is very important to a would-be leader. A friend was telling me recently about a young man who is determined to become a leading Tory politician, and during the 1974 election wrote speeches for a very eminent Member of Parliament. But my friend told me that he was completely out of touch with the ordinary man in the street and with what 'made him tick.' How can someone with no 'grass roots' experience of this sort make a successful leader?

It is true that Moses had all the advantages and privileges of a Court upbringing and education, and 'was trained in all the wisdom of the Egyptians, a powerful speaker and a man of action' (Acts 7: 22), but he knew from personal experience what it was to be poor, lonely, rejected and even 'wanted'.

But there is another temptation—perhaps that of the aspiring Labour leader, and so vividly brought out by Howard Spring in his novel, *Fame is the Spur*. It is for a man to forget the humble beginnings he has known, to affect an accent and a manner which are not natural to him, and even to despise his own past. Again, it was not so with Moses. For 'When he grew up he refused to be called the son of Pharaoh's daughter, preferring to suffer hardship with the people of God rather than enjoy the transient pleasures of sin. He considered the stigma that rests on God's anointed greater wealth than the treasures of Egypt.' (Hebrews 11: 24–26)

The great decision was made, the first vital step was

taken towards the spiritual leadership: that is, whole-hearted surrender to the purpose and will of God.

The second step followed almost at once; for we read that 'it came into his heart to visit his brethren, the children of Israel.' (Acts 7: 23) What he saw roused such compassion and anger that he knew at once where his life's work lay—in seeking to bring relief to their suffering. Unfortunately he took the law into his own hands, slew an oppressive Egyptian and, when the murder was discovered, was forced to flee the country.

It was while he was in the lonely Sinai desert, waiting for the hue and cry to subside, that God began to prepare and equip him, as He has so often done to others, for his life's work. To quote again from Churchill's essay, 'Every prophet has to come from civilization, but every prophet has to go into the wilderness. He must have a strong impression of a complex society and all that it has to give, and then he must serve periods of isolation and meditation.' It was there that great hopes and ideas began to mature in the mind of Moses and he came to realize that the time for reformation was past and that the only hope for God's people lay in liberation. It was there, too, before the burning bush that was not consumed, that he learnt something of the unquenchable love of God; and it was there that he received and finally accepted the call of God to challenge the political might and authority of Egypt.

It is interesting to note what a vital part solitude plays in the lives of great men and women. It is there, while they are alone, that great thoughts come to them and what Wordsworth calls the 'impulses of deeper birth'. As a keen gardener, I often catch myself becoming so busy in the garden itself that I never get time to enjoy it, to absorb it or to let it work in me. What the world needs today is not more action, but more thought, and the leader must learn to oscillate easily and naturally between isolation and involvement. Jesus Himself set the finest example of this, moving with perfect, automatic transmission from the mountain to the valley; and we may be sure that much of Moses' later success stemmed from those long years of solitude.

There followed the long drawn out duel with Pharaoh, with its plagues of increasing severity, the final dramatic exodus, and the adventures, victories and setbacks in the wilderness, culminating, under his successor Joshua, in the invasion of the Promised Land.

In comparing Moses with Joseph, it is interesting to note that Moses' faults and failings are far more obvious, and paradoxically it is by studying these rather than his virtues, that we arrive at a fair estimate of his greatness as a leader.

First of all, he was a very passionate man. We have already seen this in the misguided way in which he killed the Egyptian; and on at least two other occasions his temper got the better of him—when he was provoked by the stubbornness of the people into smashing the tablets of stone (Exodus 32: 19), and when he smote the rock instead of speaking to it, as he had been told to do (Numbers 20: 8–11).

I have always found that one of the hardest things in life is to move slowly when I feel strongly, and to resist the temptation to seize the telephone at once, or to write the instant, impulsive letter. Like Moses, I have had to learn that events must be given time to mature and situations to ripen before action is called for. We are told that there is 'a time to keep silence' as well as 'a time to speak' (Ecclesiastes 3: 7); and while I have rarely regretted keeping silent, I have often regretted speaking out of turn. This is perhaps one of the most elementary lessons a would-be leader has to learn—not to take the attractive short cuts to achieve what you may know to be right. Poor Moses had to learn it at great cost, and his impetuosity put the clock back a number of years.

It is interesting, too, how many great leaders have been

men whose anger, once roused, was terrible to behold; but it is not altogether surprising. Men and women who feel deeply and passionately about some cause will often speak 'unadvisedly' as Moses did (Psalm 106: 33), and sometimes act rashly as well. It was because Moses was so desperately concerned for the welfare of his people that he killed the Egyptian; and because he was so jealous for God's holiness that he broke the tablets and struck the rock.

There is a passage in C. S. Lewis' book *The Great Divorce* in which he depicts a lizard riding on a man's shoulder, representing lust, and whispering temptation in his ear. Finally the man allows it to be killed, only to find that it has been transformed into a glorious stallion, on which he himself rides into the future.

Perhaps the wonder in Moses' case was not that the lizard existed or spoke, but that the transforming process was as complete as it was. The occasional lapses only serve to highlight the extraordinary patience he displayed with people who exhibited every possible human failing, and whose ingratitude towards Moses and God was so great that they actually wished themselves back again in the land of Egypt.

Just as anger may be compassion that has been allowed to grow rancid, so diffidence is a form of sour humility; and Moses was surprisingly diffident. When God called him to his great task, he kept asking 'Who am I'? God could have flattered him: 'Moses, you are the man I have been preparing all these years for this work,' but He did not. He said in effect, 'You are asking the wrong question. It is not who you are that counts, but who I am and I will certainly be with you.'

'But', persisted Moses, 'they won't believe me.' Very patiently, God demonstrated the power that He would put at Moses' disposal. He produced and then enabled him to destroy perhaps the two most dreaded scourges in the Middle East—leprosy and snakes

(Exodus 4). A God who could do these things would in the end be believed and obeyed.

But still Moses was reluctant, and this time he pleaded his lack of eloquence in spite of what others said about his ability as a speaker. This time God's anger was aroused, but again he met Moses' condition and allowed Aaron his brother to accompany him as an official spokesman before Pharaoh.

While the ability to speak well in public is undoubtedly an advantage to a leader, and a gift which can be studied and cultivated, it would be a mistake to regard it as essential. For several years I worked under a man who never spoke in public, but whose wise and friendly counsel made him everywhere acceptable as a Christian leader. The 'Whips' in Parliament are men chosen for their unique ability to command respect and allegiance, and yet they never speak. And it is refreshing to remember that even as great an orator as Winston Churchill once had a complete black-out during a speech he was making as a young man, and sat down in apologetic confusion. Aaron may have had more to say, but Moses remained the unquestioned leader.

But slowly and surely Moses' confidence grew. Perhaps one reason why there had to be so many plagues was that it could do so and that he could become fully assured of God's presence and power. His diffidence gradually matured into humility—a quiet dependence upon God for the help that is needed; and the final verdict is interesting. 'Now the man Moses was very meek, above all the men which were upon the face of the earth' (Numbers 12: 3).

Diffidence or self-depreciation is not the same thing as meekness. Self-depreciation is the lizard that has to be destroyed; meekness is the stallion that rises from the ashes. It is a sober assessment of the gifts which God has given us, and a dependence upon Him to use them. Meekness is the opposite of pride. A man who has a very valuable Stradivarius is not being proud if he admits the fact, but only if he pretends that he can play it as well as Yehudi Menuhin.

Moses' third mistake was to try to do too much himself. He was reluctant to delegate. This is the occupational disease of leaders. It does not always stem from personal pride, at least not consciously so, but sometimes from the fact that we know we can do something better and more quickly than anyone else, and that it saves time and trouble to get on with the job ourselves. Again, Moses was a man of immense authority and moral stature, and he may have felt that to ask others to share his responsibility was a sign that he was shirking it himself. But such a policy of course is unwise and short-sighted. It means that we wear ourselves out more quickly and it also means that we never train others in the art of leadership; for the best way of doing this is to allow them to see, then to share and finally to take over some of our own responsibilities. This is often a far richer reward than praise or promotion or even higher pay, because it shows that they are not only being used but trusted.

Moses fortunately learnt this lesson fairly early on in his career and he learnt it from, of all unlikely people, his father-in-law Jethro. It was certainly one of the most important lessons he ever grasped. It meant that men like Caleb and Joshua were prepared to take over from him when his career ended; and it meant that at the ripe old age of 120, despite a long, vigorous and demanding life, we read that 'His eye was not dimmed, nor his natural force abated.' (Deuteronomy 34: 7)

If Joseph illustrated the particular qualities of leadership, it is perhaps from Moses that we learn of its special temptations. He reminds us how easy it is to grow impatient with people and want to move ahead of God, setting the pace ourselves instead of allowing Him to do so. He shows us how natural it is to shrink from the demanding challenge which we feel will tax us beyond our powers, and to ask if there is no one else who can do it; and how human and yet how contradictory, having decided that we can act, to suppose that we can do everything on our own!

It was not so much his mastery of Pharaoh and of the Children of Israel that made Moses such a great leader, as his self-mastery—his ability, that is, to conquer his temptations and outgrow his weaknesses. He learnt how to feel passionately, and yet to keep his temper. He learnt how to be meek, without becoming diffident or even cowardly. He learnt how to wield authority in a tolerant and responsible way.

Discussion Points

1. Which quality in the life of Moses does the New Testament rank most highly? And in what ways did it show itself? (See Hebrews 11: 23–29)
2. How far should background, upbringing and training be allowed to influence people in the choice of their careers?
3. Why is it sometimes so difficult to delegate work and responsibility to others? What advice would you give to someone who is seriously overworking because he insists on doing everything himself?
4. Is there such a thing as 'righteous indignation'? And if so, what are its limits?
5. If, like Moses, a Christian today lacks the confidence to speak in public, should he try to overcome this, or should he take the line that speaking just isn't his gift?
6. Apart from Moses, what other examples can you find in the Bible of the maxim that 'God matches His moments with His men'?

3. Joshua—The Commander-in-Chief

It can never be easy for someone to occupy the role of 'Heir Apparent,' and that is what Joshua was for many years—the chosen successor of Moses. In some respects he was fortunate, because although Moses was 120 years old before he died, he was full of life and vigour to the end; and Joshua himself was to last another forty years.

But he might have been much less lucky. I can think of men and women who have held on too long to the position of leadership which they first occupied in their prime. Not only have they exercised an increasingly fumbling and uncertain control over affairs, but their 'Heirs Apparent', waiting in the wings, have tended to run to seed, losing their first vision and enthusiasm, and taking over when they themselves are past their best.

There are examples of this in church, in school and in government. Perhaps the most obvious political one was the succession of Sir Anthony Eden to the premiership in 1955. Despite failing health and hints that the time had come for him to resign, Sir Winston Churchill clung to office until he was in his eighty-first year. The result was that when Eden, already a sick man, finally took over, his leadership seemed in the opinion of many to be marked by an almost feverish impatience resulting in the disastrous Suez enterprise of 1956.

If any should read this who are reaching the end of their term of office or their career, they should resist the temptation to hold on that little bit longer. Go before rather than after ill health or old age force you to retire.

Go while there is still energy and strength enough for further useful service, perhaps in some other sphere. Go even if you think the man destined to succeed you is raw and unready, remembering that your own departure may give him the chance to mature which your overwhelming presence, like some great beech tree, has so far prevented.

King David made this mistake. Instead of abdicating in favour of his son Solomon, he held on too long. The result was that, only by some very adroit last minute action, was a *coup d'état* prevented and his rightful heir established on the throne. What has been called 'the grace of retirement' is a fairly rare virtue.

The clergy used to be particular offenders in this respect. Lack of money and having nowhere else to live meant that many benefices were filled with septuagenarian or even octogenarian incumbents who could only be removed if they were proved to be 'crooks, crocks or cranks', and then not without great difficulty. It was this situation, now happily much improved, which led to the remark attributed I believe to Dr. Donald Coggan, the present Archbishop of Canterbury, *à propos* some elderly and inflexibly rooted vicar: 'Never mind, while there is death, there is hope.'

But perhaps you yourself are an 'heir apparent', ready to take over from someone else the running of that meeting, committee or department. Already it seems that you have been waiting for ages. You feel rather like a man who has sat all day in the pavilion with his pads on, waiting for the next wicket to fall, and wondering whether he is ever going to get an innings at all.

If you are in this position, you may be tempted to be impatient, and to allow your impatience to boil over into resentment, criticism and bitterness. Worse still, you may be tempted to be disloyal, and even to intrigue in an unworthy manner for the removal of the man who stands in your way. Both temptations must be resisted, as we can be sure that Joshua resisted them. Never pluck the apple. Wait for it to fall.

But it is doubtful whether this was Joshua's problem. With, as it turned out, forty years still to go, he was probably glad not to have succeeded earlier and grateful for every minute he had to prepare himself. But he did have another problem; for it is never easy to succeed a really great man. 'You simply can't go wrong,' we sometimes say to a man who is taking over from someone who has been a disappointing failure; but the opposite is true if the man you are following has been a resounding success. How can you possibly live up to his standard?

This was Joshua's problem. Think of it! Moses' successor! How could he possibly cope? The first secret of his success seems to have been that *he knew himself.* He had a proper estimate of his weaknesses and capabilities. He knew that it would be as easy to try to follow slavishly in the footsteps of Moses as it would be to work in a way diametrically opposed. He would be neither a reactionary nor a revolutionary.

Moses had been a great administrator and judge; Joshua was a soldier. Moses had created a nation. Joshua must settle and establish it within its own frontiers. Moses had organized and trained the people. Joshua must subdue their enemies. Moses wielded a pen; Joshua a sword. And so from the start the pattern was quite clear. The days of wandering in the wilderness were over, and the invasion of the promised land had begun under a new but well-tried commander.

And what a brilliant commander he became! To match his exploits we would need to read of the triumphs of Marlborough or Wellington, or in more recent times of Rommel and Montgomery. Jericho, Ai, the Gibeonites, the Amorites—these were just some of the cities and tribes that fell before him, and the scenes of his spectacular military achievements. How splendidly he fulfilled God's purpose for him, and how sad it would have been if a slavish devotion to the memory and methods of Moses had prevented him from becoming his real self!

He was a born soldier, just as Moses was a born statesman, and one of the first and most important things about leadership is to be sure that we are exercising it in the right direction. We must beware, for example, in choosing a career of doing the expected thing and taking the line of least resistance, following the pattern marked out perhaps by family or predecessors. Because we come of a long line of soldiers, it does not follow that God wants us in the army. On the other hand, to quote Field-Marshal Montgomery, 'My father had always hoped I would be a clergyman. That didn't happen and I well recall his disappointment when I told him that I wanted to be a soldier.' Few would question that Monty made the right choice. He knew himself, his capacity and ability, better than anyone else could possibly do.

It was Moses himself who first discovered Joshua, and under God chose him to be a leader (Deuteronomy. 31: 3). He appointed him when little more than a boy as his A.D.C. It was Joshua who won the famous victory against the Amalekites (Exodus 17); and he was still only twenty-five when he established himself firmly as a leader-to-be at the famous Council of War at Kadesh-Barnea.

The occasion was the return of the twelve spies from the promised land, one man representing each tribe, and Joshua being the representative of Ephraim. One by one, these men rose to give their long gloomy reports until a point was reached when Caleb and Joshua could stand it no longer. We can picture Caleb, the older man, leaping to his feet, banging the table with his fist, and declaring that they were fully capable of invading the country, capturing Jericho and establishing themselves in the land of Canaan. Together they pleaded and argued but it was no good. The people threatened to stone them and they were only saved by the intervention of the Lord himself (Numbers 13 and 14).

All this time Moses had been in the Chair, and he saw that if D-day was to take place at all, there could only be one commander. Caleb, some fifteen years the elder, was probably ruled out by age and that left Joshua the son of Nun as the one and only answer.

Two things must have impressed Moses about Joshua, as indeed they impress us. First he was no defeatist. He was not just prepared to sit back and let things take their course. For far too long the Israelites had been dithering about in the wilderness wasting their time and losing their morale. Action was called for—action this day; and if this meant the end of peaceful co-existence with hostile tribes, then that was the price they must pay.

And he was no pessimist either. He refused to believe in the possibilities of defeat. For him they did not exist. He knew that with God all things are possible and that the God of the Red Sea could be the God of the Jordan. To every criticism and to every cautious warning he had but one answer, 'We are well able to overcome.'

This leads on to the second secret of Joshua's success as a leader—*he knew Moses*. As we have seen, from the early days he was Moses' constant companion, and we can guess what courage, wisdom and patience he must have absorbed from the older man. I have often thought what a privilege it would be to have lived in the company of some great person. It would have been impossible, for example, to have known Socrates without some of his wisdom rubbing off, or not to have been infected by Napoleon's courage or Shakespeare's genius. There was in fact a little-known poet of the last century on whose tombstone were inscribed the words, 'He was a friend of Keats'. That is all he is remembered for. But what a privilege! And that is how Joshua must have felt. 'He was a friend of Moses.'

Like Joshua, every great leader has once been and must

always remain a learner. You cannot become the first unless you have been the second. As we have seen, Joshua was fortunate enough to have as his teacher one of the greatest men of all time. So was Solomon. So was Elisha. But this is not always the case, and quite often a future leader has learnt the most important secrets from a humble, obscure and not very distinguished friend of his youth.

And the good leader never stops being a learner. As soon as he does, his influence wanes and he becomes at best stale and at worst inflexible and even arrogant. He will learn from the past. He will learn from his friends. He will learn, and this is perhaps the hardest of all, from his subordinates and even from those with whom he disagrees, and who oppose him. As Oscar Wilde said, 'A man cannot be too careful in the choice of his enemies, for they often teach us more than our friends.'

It often surprises and even frightens me to discover how easily and often unwittingly people can be influenced. A chance remark is repeated with an authority we never intended it to have, or a mannerism is imitated, or a habit copied. Although we are unaware of it, probably most of us are setting an example to someone else, and providing a model for speech and behaviour. This is a responsibility we cannot avoid, for 'none of us lives to himself' (Romans 14: 7) and in a small way we are all leaders.

It is interesting to reflect that there were nearly fifty years between the ages of Moses and Joshua, but age need be nothing like the barrier that is sometimes supposed. It may seem to be so for a time, but the older one grows in body very often the younger one becomes in spirit. I remember that very experienced Christian leader, Dr. Max Warren, once telling me that in his experience he found that, as he got older, he grew towards the young and enjoyed a greater rapport with them at forty than he did at twenty-five. Perhaps this is why the generation gap seems to narrow with age, and children sometimes have a greater affinity with their grandparents than with their own parents.

To the young aspiring leader the message is this: don't make the mistake which Rehoboam made (1 Kings 12). Don't despise the advice of the elderly. Their experience may be just what is needed to temper your energy and enthusiasm. Their dreams will mellow your visions. Their very detachment is an advantage. 'All passion spent' and with no lingering ambitions of their own, they can look calmly and objectively on the problems which involve the leader. We talk of people mellowing with age. They ought to do so. Tolerance, flexibility, sympathy— these are the attitudes of the very old just as sometimes they are the things which the very young may lack.

There was yet a third secret of Joshua's outstanding success. He knew himself. He knew Moses, but most important of all *he knew God*. He had probably done so most of his life, but just before his first real test as a leader, on the outskirts of Jericho he had an experience he never forgot (Joshua 5: 13–15). In some ways it was like the vision that Moses had before the burning bush at the time of his own commissioning.

As Joshua approached the city, he saw a man standing in front of him with a drawn sword in his hand. He challenged him, 'Are you for us or for our enemies?' and the man said to him, 'I am here as the captain of the army of the Lord.' The irony is delightful. Joshua must have felt like a school boy on his way to watch Yorkshire play cricket who asks a stranger whether he is a Yorkshire supporter, only to receive the reply 'I am Geoff Boycott.'

His whole attitude changed at once. 'What have you to say to your servant, my lord?' he asked. Immediately he was the subordinate, a mere soldier in the army of the Lord; and this vital lesson of humility he had to learn before the siege of Jericho began and the campaigns that followed.

Then 'the captain of the Lord's army said to him "Take off your sandals; the place where you are standing is holy"; and Joshua did so'. What a strange command for a soldier to be given! We would have expected him to be told to 'put on the whole armour of God, to gird himself for battle, to take up the weapons of his warfare,' but no. First he must take off, and only then can he put on.

In other words, as well as humility there must be holiness. These were the twin secrets of victory which Joshua had to learn. They were the same as the lessons Moses learnt, and every great leader from then onwards. No matter what gifts God has given us, no matter how rich and varied the advice and counsel we have received from others the thing that counts most is our relationship to the Captain himself: a relationship symbolized in the case of Joshua by the bowed head and the bare feet. The question is not whether God is on our side, but whether we are on his.

Discussion Points

1. What great promises did Joshua receive at the start of his career as Commander-in-Chief? (See Joshua 1).
2. Can you see from Joshua 1 and from other parts of the Bible (for example, Isaiah 41: 10, Psalm 27: 14; 56: 3, John 16: 33, Acts 27: 23, 24, 1 Peter 3: 14–17, 1 John 5: 4) some of the secrets of spiritual and moral courage?
3. How can we benefit in practice from the help which the older generation of Christians is able to give?
4. How can we inspire those we lead with enthusiasm for God's work?
5. Is it possible to succeed an outstanding personality without slavish imitation or foolish reaction?
6. 'Never pluck an apple. Wait for it to fall' (see page 21). Should Christians always follow this advice?

4. Samson—The Resistance Leader

The Children of Israel were suffering a time of miserable humiliation. The great hostile power to the south-west, Philistia, had invaded their country and subjugated its people. They were enduring the sort of fate we have seen in recent years meted out to countries like Tibet, Hungary and Czechoslovakia. For forty years this humiliation lasted, and the historian referred to the period as 'the days of the Philistines'.

Most people accepted it. They did not feel inclined to disturb the status quo. Perhaps they were afraid of reprisals, and in any case it was better to be 'red' than 'dead'. 'Knowest thou not that the Philistines are rulers over us?' (Judges 15: 11), they asked any who challenged this servile spirit of subjection. Co-existence was probably the polite word for this attitude; collaboration was the other.

Everywhere you went you would breathe the rank, rotten, foetid air of pessimism and defeat. Morale had reached its lowest point. But there was one man who was different—one strong, young figure who stood out against the drawling tides of drift and surrender, of faint endeavour and feeble impulse; and his name was Samson.

Like other famous characters in the Bible, such as Isaac and John the Baptist, he was born in fulfilment of a specific promise. He was yet another example of the principle we have already noted, that God matches His moments with His men. The need arises, the crisis appears and there to meet it with God's help is Joseph or Daniel, Luther or Wesley. With God it is never 'jobs for the boys', but 'boys for the jobs'. And here again was a national emergency, and here to meet it was a man of destiny, the child of wise and loving parents, the product of a God-fearing home.

The name 'Samson' means 'Little Sun', or 'Sun One', or as we might say today, 'Sunshine'. It was a singularly appropriate name, because his appearance on the scene at this dark time must have seemed like the dawn of hope to his down-trodden and discouraged fellow-countrymen.

Again and again we read of Samson that 'the Spirit of the Lord came upon him', and when He did so, Samson was irresistible. There was an occasion when he met a lion in the street, and with his own bare hands he tore it apart as if it had been a chicken. It was to Samson again that we owe what has come to be known as the 'scorched earth policy'. He harnessed together a battalion of foxes, some three hundred in number, and tying torches to their tails, sent them screaming and blazing through the enemy cornfields.

Outnumbered by no fewer than a thousand to one, he did not take to the hills or the forests, but challenged his opponents to personal combat. And what weapons did he choose? Nuclear bombs? Germ warfare? Inter-continental ballistic missiles? Nothing more lethal than the jaw-bone of a dead donkey. Finally, when his enemies thought they had him trapped in Gaza, and shut the city gates on him, he waited till midnight, and not only made his escape, but carried away the city gates, posts and all, and planted them on the neighbouring hills of Hebron.

What a man! For him there could be no peaceful co-existence with his country's enemies. It was war to the bitter end. Of course he was a child of his times. He lived in days when success was measured in casualties rather than in converts; but he was very much more than a sort of Old Testament James Bond. He did much solid and useful work. He raised the morale of his fellow-country-men, and for twenty years governed Israel and led their resistance to the Philistine occupation. He gave the enemy no respite. Small wonder that they should refer to him as 'the destroyer of our country'!

I never fail to find myself moved and stirred by war-time stories of resistance movements. Even in Germany itself there were those who well before the war began were working for the overthrow of Hitler. That they failed was not due to any lack of courage on the part of men like Beck, Witzleben, Goerdeler and Stauffenberg, but partly to a series of misfortunes and partly, it must be admitted, to the total lack of any encouragement or co-operation on the part of the allies.

The Christian Church is a Resistance Movement. It fights, not for the overthrow of men, but for the over-throw of those things which so often control the hearts of men—greed, pride, selfishness and envy. But how badly it needs leaders—men and women who will stand up and be counted! Nothing is easier than to drift with the tide, to 'co-exist' with the standards and values of the present day, and to acquiesce weakly with those who seek to undermine the Christian principles on which society is built.

Of course we must be careful that we are fighting the real enemy and not just shadow-boxing. It is a great mistake, for example, for more traditionally-minded Christians to see any special virtue in the habits and conventions of dress, hair-style and speech in which they themselves have been brought up. Every class has its particular culture, and a new Christian should not be made to feel that he must change that class any more than he has to change his nationality. As St. Paul says, 'Each one must order his life according to . . . his condi-tion when God called him' (1 Corinthians 7: 17), and not try to be someone different.

On the other hand, it is equally wrong to dismiss Christian virtues as invalid just because in the past they have been associated with the middle-classes. There is a tendency for this to happen. As a recent article in *The Times* put it, 'it has been possible to ridicule almost anything, from ordinary courtesy to a respect for disciplined learning, family life or national institutions, by a pejorative reference to them as "middle-class".'

We are living in a world which belongs to God, and Christians of all classes must recognize where the real forces of evil lie, and refuse to co-operate with them. Wherever we have influence—in our homes or our jobs, on radio or television, in parliament or press, we must do all we can to sabotage the strongholds which Satan has established for himself. It is an unpopular, risky and even dangerous way of life, and we shall need all the courage and determination of Samson to do it.

But at the height of his power, Samson failed. Something went wrong. Suddenly this magnificent champion, seemingly in full and irresistible flight, was seen to stall, to struggle for a moment, and then to crash to the ground. What had happened? It was the old, sad story. Not once, but many times in history, the enemy has used the charms of a beautiful woman to extract military secrets from a brave but undisciplined soldier who has the arm of a warrior, but the eye of a philanderer. 'Tell me,' said Delilah, 'tell me, I pray thee, wherein thy great strength lieth.' He played for time. He parried. He pretended. But it was no good. 'Delilah pressed him daily with her words,' and, hopelessly outflanked, undermined and seduced, 'he told her all his heart' (Judges 16: 6–20).

The secret was out. The code was cracked. 'If I be shaven, then my strength will go from me, and I shall be weak, and like any other man.' There lay the bitter, tragic irony—'like any other man'. God meant Samson to be different from other men. He was a Nazarite, a spiritual commando, a man chosen and equipped for special service. The very word itself means 'different' or 'separate', and now he was to be 'like any other man'.

Robert Browning has a pathetic little poem called

The Lost Leader. 'Just for a handful of silver he left us, just for a riband to stick on his coat.' There is perhaps no greater tragedy than the failure of a leader, the discovery that the person we have admired, respected and followed has feet of clay. That is the true tragedy in the lives of Saul, of Julius Caesar, of Parnell. That was the danger Paul was so acutely aware of when he prayed that having sought to lead others he might not himself be rejected— like the driving instructor who fails to pass his own test.

We must not imagine for a moment that promotion brings immunity from temptation—rather the reverse. The leader is particularly vulnerable. To begin with, Satan knows that if he can topple him then he can bring about the downfall of others. Then his very position leaves him exposed, lonely and isolated. He becomes the object of flattery and a target for place-seekers and suckers. He finds that he is his own master, and can 'get away with' what would be checked and discovered among his inferiors; for 'quis custodiet ipsos custodes'? And if he fails, he can expect no mercy from his fellowmen, for there is nothing that a scandal-loving press enjoys more than exposing the private lives of public men. No wonder that we are told to pray 'for all that are in authority' (1 Timothy 2: 1, 2)! Such people need our prayers and our sympathy.

But let us examine a little more closely the nature of Samson's failure. A Nazarite made three vows: never to touch a dead body or anything unclean; never to take strong drink, even vinegar or raisins; never to cut his hair. The first stood for inner purity, the second for separation from the heathen cults among which he lived, and the third for dedication to God. One by one Samson allowed these great arsenals of his religion to be overrun. There was the dead lion, and the honey he extracted from its carcase. There was the great carousel at the time of his wedding. And now this final strand was snapped, when he allowed his hair to be cut.

Samson was like a chess-player in a winning position, but who had grown careless. First he lost a knight, then a castle and now finally his queen. He hadn't a chance. His position was hopeless. He had lost too much spiritual blood.

Someone has said that there is no greater gift that a spiritual leader can make to his followers than his own personal holiness. Nothing can be a substitute for that. He may be a born organizer, a daring, inspiring and imaginative pioneer, but unless his followers can look up to him spiritually, all these other qualities count for nothing. It was here that Samson's failure was so tragic and so total.

It is here, too, that some may take courage. They may feel they lack some of the more obvious marks of leadership. They do not speak particularly well, nor are they noted for administrative ability or strength of personality. But these things count for very little when measured against the spiritual qualities of holiness of life and consecration to the Lord; for if Christian leadership means anything at all, it means that people are helped to see Christ more clearly than before.

Happily that is not quite the end of the story. We might call the opening chapter of his life *Sunrise* and chapter two *Power-cut*. But there was a third and final chapter—*Come-back*. It was in this respect that he differed most markedly from that other great Old Testament disappointment—King Saul. He had a second chance.

'Eyeless in Gaza, at the mill with slaves,' this great pathetic giant, now a blinded prisoner and slave, was given the task of grinding corn for his captors. But as he did so, his hair began to grow again. More important still, he turned back again to the God whom he had failed and dishonoured. 'O Lord God, remember me, I pray Thee, and strengthen me, I pray Thee, only this once, O God.' (Judges 16: 28)

The great strength that had drained so suddenly and dramatically began to flow back. Why his captors allowed it to happen, we cannot say. Perhaps they thought that as a blind man he presented no problems and held no fears for them. Perhaps by keeping him as a kind of pet performer (for his strength was still considerable) they found that he amused and distracted the people, earning foreign currency, no doubt, at the same time. Whatever the reason, they lived to regret. it.

What marvellous film material the closing scene! We can see the great festival hall crammed to the doors with the noble, the rich and the influential. It is the Première, the First Night, the Command Performance at which this fabulous strong man, this astonishing war trophy, is going to display his titanic strength. Little did they guess how he would do it! The horny fingers clutched at the great stone pillars, the muscles tightened, and the huge shoulders began to heave with enormous power. The building quivered, tottered, and crashed to the ground, bringing Samson and his countrymen a greater triumph than they had ever enjoyed in battle; for, as the historian laconically remarks, 'so the dead which he slew at his death were more than they which he slew in his life.' (Judges 16: 30)

'Why', it may be asked, 'has Samson been included in this portrait gallery of great spiritual leaders? What qualifies him for a place?' I think there are three answers. He provides us with an example, a warning and an encouragement.

None who aspire to leadership can ignore his daring and his panache. He led men, not from the desk or the rostrum, but from the front. His methods may have been crude, his judgements immature, but there could be no doubting his total dedication to the destruction of the enemy.

Then what went wrong? He grew careless. He relaxed his guard. And no leader can afford to do these things.

For as we have seen, a leader is especially vulnerable, simply because Satan, if he can cause his downfall, can damage God's work so widely, and give the enemies of the Lord a chance to gloat and blaspheme.

But the life of Samson ends on a positive, encouraging note. The prayer—'remember me'—speaks volumes. To 'remember' is the opposite of 'dismember'. Samson had got out of touch, out of joint with the Lord, out of gear. He needed to be re-membered. The branch needed to be grafted into the main stem once again, so that the power could flow to its furthest extremities. Samson reminds us that even if leaders fail—and from time to time some tragic case arises of a Christian leader who has come a moral and spiritual crash—this need not be the end. David proved it. Simon Peter proved it. Samson proved it. There is forgiveness, and even better than that, there can open up to the re-membered servant fields of usefulness which he thought were closed for ever.

It is here, of course, that society can be so brutal. It will not allow a man to bury his past and to make a fresh start. How differently God treats us! 'As far as the east is from the west, so far hath He removed our transgressions from us.' (Psalm 103: 12) He puts them out of sight, out of reach and out of mind. He is infinitely merciful, and there are many Christians around today, doing splendid work for Him, all the more humbly and wisely, perhaps, because He has helped them to recover from some moral or spiritual disaster.

Discussion Points

1. What lessons in resisting temptation had Samson failed to learn? (Matthew 26: 41, Romans 13: 14, 1 Peter 5: 6–9). What are the Tempter's most successful techniques?
2. 'Cast down, but not cast out.' How far does that

describe the life of Samson? (Micah 7: 8, John 6: 37, Psalm 51, Isaiah 55: 7).

3. We read that 'the Spirit of the Lord came mightily upon Samson' (Judges 14: 6). In practical terms what does that mean for us today?

4. Is it ever right for a Christian to resist authority?

5. How can we best help a friend who has failed badly as a Christian?

6. 'God may forgive me, but I can never forgive myself.' Is that a Christian sentiment?

5. Samuel—The Archbishop

This is a title which we might I think reasonably apply to Samuel, though in a mediaeval rather than a modern sense; for he was a political as well as a religious figure, comparable in status perhaps to Cardinal Wolsey at the time of Henry VIII or Archbishop Makarios in recent years. He was the last of the great judges and the first in a long line of prophets.

At the time of his birth, Israel was in very poor shape. For forty years Eli had ruled the country, but he was now ninety-eight years old, quite blind, and had completely lost his grip. His sons Hophni and Phinehas ('so crooked that you could hide them behind a spiral staircase') were totally unfitted to succeed him, and bribery and corruption flourished on every side.

Not only was the country in moral chaos domestically, but the great hostile power of Philistia lurked menacingly on the south-west border, ready to take advantage of the first signs of weakness and invade and subjugate her traditional enemy.

In fact, the land was crying out for a new strong lead and for fresh hands to take over the reins of government. It needed a second Moses. This was the world into which Samuel was born; and he was destined to be God's man to match the moment.

He began with one tremendous advantage. He had a God-fearing mother who prayed for him. There is, of course, no law of spiritual inheritance. We are expressly told that the Christian faith is not transmitted genetically. The new birth is 'not of blood, nor of the will of the flesh' (John 1: 12, 13). But at the same time godly parents can create an environment in which children may be brought up to know and love the Lord. Indeed, it has been said that 'the proper time to influence the character of a child is about a hundred years before it is born'.

Then why does it not always work? Why were Eli's sons such disastrous failures, and even Samuel's little better? A lifetime of work amongst children and teenagers has brought me no firm answers to questions like these. Sometimes I think that the children of Christian families, looking back, feel that their parents were over-anxious for their spiritual welfare, and tried to give them too much too soon. Sunday, for example, was a negative and restricted day. Conversation at meals lacked breadth and humour; and the kind of entertainment provided and encouraged was tepid and old-fashioned compared with what they found in the homes of their friends. Sir Edmund Gosse, in his book *Father and Son*, provides the extreme and classical example of this kind of mistaken pressure.

But if that was the sort of mistake that people were apt to make a generation ago, perhaps the danger today lies if anything at the opposite extreme. The home can be too relaxed. There is an absence of discipline, and parents sometimes fail to give a positive lead, perhaps because they are afraid of being thought authoritarian. The result is that their children do not appreciate Christian standards and values, and these things do not form the framework of their upbringing as they should. This was clearly where Eli went wrong.

But I have never been able to find a formula or a perfect recipe for the Christian upbringing of children, and it is a process beyond all others in which parents need to be spiritually sensitive. Somewhere perhaps the perfect balance is to be found, but all we really know is that some (the great majority in my experience) succeed like

Hannah; while others suffer the bitter disappointment of Eli and Samuel himself.

There is something whimsical about the child Samuel being left in the care of a man only two years short of a hundred, but there seems to have been a rapport between them; for Eli still had much to give and no doubt Samuel owed a great deal to his ancient tutor.

Few people are fortunate enough to be able to choose a school for their children, and many think that none should have that privilege, regarding equality as more important than freedom. But where this is possible, Christian parents rightly feel that they are acting in the best interests of their children if they can find a school where Christian influences are at work.

The home, the school and the church are, as they always have been, the most important influences during the formative years of a child's life; and first Hannah and then Eli and the worshipping community at Shiloh prepared Samuel for the call that came to him as a boy and the life of service that followed; for we are told that 'Samuel grew, and the Lord was with him and did let none of his words fall to the ground' (1 Samuel 3: 19).

The years that followed marked the saddest and most bitter in the history of Israel—invasion, subjugation and desecration—and it seemed as if the life of the nation could never revive. The historian, in fact, can hardly bring himself to write of this period, and it is left to Asaph in a mournful poem (Psalm 78) to sing of his country's grief and anguish.

But very slowly things began to improve and that they did so was due to one man—Samuel—who for twenty-five years ruled the country, its greatest judge since Moses.

His leadership was felt chiefly in three directions. Spiritually he called the people back from the wicked idolatry they had practised for so long, promising God's help and deliverance on condition of national repentance (1 Samuel 7: 3).

Perhaps the greatest thing he did for his people was to pray for them. Just as Hannah had prayed for him, so he prayed for his country. 'God forbid,' he said, 'that I should sin against the Lord in ceasing to pray for you' (1 Samuel 12: 23). 'When I am dead,' said Mary Tudor, 'you shall find "Calais" written on my heart.' That was how Samuel felt about Israel, and he might well have echoed the words of the Psalmist 'If I forget thee, O Jerusalem, let my right hand forget her cunning' (Psalm 137: 5). The father of a friend of mine who was the vicar of a church used to spend time each week moving from pew to pew and praying by name for the people who normally occupied each place on Sunday. That was true pastoral leadership.

Now and then we meet someone who is making good progress in the Christian life, and being much used by God. We begin to make enquiries, and we find that behind the scenes there is a parent, a godparent, or perhaps a friend who is praying for him every day; and this quiet, unseen support explains everything. There is no better way in which we can help someone than by praying for him—and perhaps no harder way either.

Educationally too, Samuel introduced reforms. He founded the schools of the prophets—Bible colleges, we might almost call them—where men were trained in the knowledge of God and then sent back to farm or city understanding the nature of Jehovah, how He was to be worshipped and what sort of life His followers ought to lead.

Today there may be a decline in formal church worship, but there are parallels to what Samuel used to do. Wherever I go, I hear of groups meeting in houses for study and prayer, under the leadership of some enterprising Christian layman. The same sort of thing is happening in schools, colleges and other institutions as well, and would no doubt be more widespread still if people with courage and initiative would come forward.

Politically, he agreed after much hesitation and prayer, that the existing system of government should give way to a properly constituted monarchy. It involved a great risk, as he plainly told the people, and could only be regarded as a second-best choice to satisfy a nation as yet unfitted for its true destiny, which was to be a theocracy, that is to own the undisputed sovereignty of God Himself.

It cannot have been an easy decision for him personally, for it meant stepping down and allowing someone else to take his place. But he was an old man now, his sons had proved themselves totally unfitted for high office, and it seemed that, humanly speaking, a monarchy was the only way of guaranteeing the future of the nation.

Once this decision was made, all Samuel's energies were directed to choosing and training and assisting the new king, and the final phase of his life centres upon Saul. Samuel the judge becomes Samuel the king-maker.

Disappointment dogged Samuel all through his life. Eli was a disappointment, then his sons, and now Saul. The start was so promising, for Saul seemed every inch a king. Where the trouble began, it is hard to say, but there are people who cannot assume power without becoming proud, arrogant, contemptuous and despotic; and it seems to have been like that with Saul. In fact, it is probably that he actually did suffer from some form of paranoia—not an unknown condition among people when power goes to their heads. In his better moments he recognized this, as we see from the tragic epitaph he prepared for himself when he spoke with David for the last time, 'I have sinned . . . I have played the fool, and have erred exceedingly' (1 Samuel 26: 21).

It is here that we see Samuel in his third role—pupil, reformer and now counsellor; and we can tell how highly Saul regarded him in this respect by the way in which he tried to seek his advice after his death when he resorted to the witch at Endor (1 Samuel 28).

Perhaps one of the least appreciated but most important tasks of a leader is to advise and even control the man who is at the summit. It only became apparent some years after the war how much Winston Churchill owed to Lord Allanbrooke; and from reading the life of Stanley Baldwin (who incidentally started every day with prayer) it is evident with what tact and firmness he sought to guide King Edward VIII in the fateful decisions that he had to make at the time of the abdication in 1936.

It has been said that every great man has some confidant to whom he turns for counsel and advice—some remote parish parson perhaps, to whom an important bishop will make secret pilgrimages to ask for wisdom and guidance; and to be the sort of person to whom others turn for advice when they have critical decisions to make, is to be a leader of a most responsible kind.

That was Samuel's responsibility and one that he discharged with great faithfulness, just as Nathan did to David and many years later Isaiah to King Hezekiah. It is difficult to see how he could have succeeded, given Saul's intransigence; but long after Saul had been rejected by God, after their personal relations were ended for ever, we are told that 'Samuel mourned for Saul' (1 Samuel 15: 3). His indignation at Saul's rebellion was tinged with an infinite feeling of sadness for what might have been.

The story of Saul is only of importance to us here in so far as it helps us to understand Samuel; but we must note in passing the calamity of another 'might-have-been'—opportunities wasted, advantages lost and promise unfulfilled. It is this that makes Saul perhaps the most tragic figure in the whole Bible, standing incongruously beside one of the greatest. They could have shared fame. They could have formed an unbeatable partnership, but it was not to be.

Samuel never lived to enjoy the fruits of his greatest success, the choice and coronation of David. Saul had

everything to commend him, David, at any rate out-
wardly, very little; but Samuel's last recorded act was to
anoint the boy and no doubt on another shore he must
have rejoiced at the triumphs of the shepherd king.

There is an irony here because it often happens that
we never know where or how we have influenced others
for God. I have been told that I owe much to the prayers
of a grandmother, and studying her carefully marked
Bible I can believe it; but she never lived to see me
become a Christian. Eli never lived to see the greatness of
Samuel, nor Samuel the greatness of David; nor David
that of Solomon. 'These all having obtained good report
through faith received not the promise . . .' (Hebrews
11: 13).

We are told little or nothing of Samuel's closing years
spent in retirement at Ramah. It cannot have been a
happy time with Saul tearing the country apart and
David a fugitive outlaw. But Samuel still retained a place
of supreme honour in the hearts of the people—the man
who had prayed for them, united them and then refused
the highest post he could have had for himself. Such
quiet, deep, unassertive leadership is not forgotten. Such
men live on in the hearts of the nation, and it is not
surprising that, at what must have been a kind of a state
funeral, the reporter tells us that 'all the Israelites
gathered together and lamented him' (1 Samuel 25: 1).

Discussion Points

1. 'The child is father to the man.' How far is this true
   spiritually? (Proverbs 22: 6, 2 Timothy 3: 15–16).
2. Can you think of other leaders who were, like Samuel,
   great men of prayer? (See, for example, Genesis
   18: 22–33, 1 Kings 18, Daniel 6: 10, John 17.)
3. Samuel was disappointed in his sons. Why? What

mistakes do parents make in their attempt to bring up children as Christians?

4. 'Samuel mourned for Saul.' How can we express our Christian love for people who have disappointed us?

5. How can we guide another, perhaps younger person, without dominating him and making him too dependent upon us?

6. Samuel changed his country's form of government. In what practical ways can the Christian help to reform Society in our country today?

6. David—The King

It was early autumn and the local farmers were just beginning to harvest their crops. David and his little party were quartered in the cave of Adullam, some twenty-five miles to the south-west of Bethlehem and not far from the frontier of Philistia. 'Besieged' would perhaps be a better word to describe their situation, for David dared not venture forth. Bethlehem itself was in the hands of the Philistines and King Saul's men were everywhere on the look-out for him. He was in fact between the devil and the deep sea.

Perhaps the nearest any of us have got to the life of a fugitive or to being 'wanted' in this sense is to have seen *The Colditz Story* on television or read an essay like Arthur Bryant's on the escape of Charles Stuart after the battle of Worcester; but it is at such times that the true worth of friendship is proved and we discover what loyalty really means.

It is at times like these, too, that a longing comes over us for the simplest and most basic things of life: for a bath, a loaf, a clean shirt or a bed. So it was with David, and one day, perhaps not expecting to be taken seriously, he cried 'If only I could have a drink of water from the well by the gate of Bethlehem!'

His remark was heard or overheard by three of his companions, and with incredible courage they made the perilous journey through the Philistine lines, drew water from what has since been called 'David's well', and brought it back to their commander. David was overcome with emotion. 'He refused to drink it; he poured it out to the Lord and said "God forbid that I should do such a thing! Can I drink the blood of these men who risked their lives for it".' (2 Samuel 23: 14–17) The courage and devotion of his followers had turned the water into blood.

This little story typifies and perhaps at the same time explains the amazing loyalty which David inspired through his own warm-hearted, generous and courageous spirit.

David's was a complex and varied career. Starting as a humble shepherd boy he ended a king; but on the way he revealed himself as a musician, poet, soldier, fugitive and exile. The range of his gifts and the variety of his experiences are almost unique, and those who want him brought to life in a new and vivid way would do well to read *The Life of David* by Duff Cooper.

It was under him that the loose aggregate of Bedouin tribes of the days of Eli became the mighty world-famous Israel under the magnificent Solomon. At first, he was only accepted by the Judaean tribes and established his kingdom at Hebron; but seven or eight years later, after the death of Saul's son Ishbosheth, he was acclaimed by the Israelites as well, and Jerusalem became his capital, where he reigned for thirty-three years. By conquests and alliances he subdued the hostile tribes around him and extended his kingdom from Egypt to the Euphrates.

What was it, we must ask, that gave him such a unique place in the history of his people? He lacked the almost guileless integrity of Joseph and the supreme authority of Moses; but he possessed to a greater degree than either of them the capacity to be loved. Moses might inspire admiration; David inspired affection. People found they could identify with him as with few others. He was 'one of them'. Moses led from above. There was an almost olympic dignity about him. David led from within, from among his people. He was the democrat while Moses was the autocrat. He was 'The people's king'.

We notice, first of all, his *humanity*. David never forgot his humble beginnings and indeed he gloried in them, giving the praise to God who had loaded him with such benefits and privileges. His tribe was obscure, his place in the family was lowly, for he was the youngest of eight children, and his occupation modest. He knew the meaning of poverty, of loneliness and even of deprivation.

And it also meant that he was vulnerable. Joseph seemed almost beyond the reach of temptation, but David possessed all those weaknesses which people so easily recognize in themselves. He could be dangerously indecisive. He was a prey to introspection. There were moments of pride, and there was the tragic episode concerning Uriah the Hittite which, even judged by the standards of those days, remains inexcusable and, in such a good man, almost inexplicable.

Nor was he a particularly good judge of men. He was apt to mis-read character, attributing evil motives where none existed, and trusting those who were unworthy of his confidence.

And yet this very humanity won the hearts of people, for they saw a reflection of themselves. He was not too good to be true, which is what we feel about some leaders; he was sometimes too true to be good.

It was perhaps because he was so natural that people loved David. He had to be himself. I remember once asking a friend how another man was getting on in a very important post to which he had just been appointed. 'He can't make up his mind which pose to adopt,' was the rather unkind and I think undeserved reply.

But I knew what he meant. I could picture a man standing in front of his mirror 'trying on' various expressions and attitudes. Should he be dignified and condescending, at the risk of being thought pompous? Should he be free-and-easy, sociable and hearty, at the risk of being thought cheap and vulgar? It is very easy for a leader to fall into this kind of trap—to be over-concerned with the impression he is creating, and to adopt a carefully studied pose.

The famous Labour leader Aneurin Bevan once turned up at a royal banquet (as he was perfectly entitled to do) in a lounge suit. Next day he was pompously ticked off by the Prime Minister, Clement Attlee. But no one at the Palace objected. Perhaps they knew how unnatural it would have been for him to do otherwise. He had to be true to himself.

And it was David's naturalness which endeared him to people. He was a bad actor. He had to be himself, even if this meant failing to camouflage his weaknesses. People found common ground with him, and felt at home, and having done so, they quickly became aware of his remarkable qualities.

They noticed first of all his outstanding *courage*. The life of a shepherd in those days was not the peaceful, idyllic existence which some painters have described, but a hard, exacting occupation which we might fairly compare with that of the coal miner of today. It was here in the lonely valleys and the deserted hills that David learnt to fear no evil, neither man nor beast. His exploits were legendary, and when as a mere youth he challenged and slew the giant Philistine Goliath his name was made for good. Nothing that happened after that could rob him of the respect and adulation which are always bestowed on the heavyweight champion of the world.

But a lot did happen and it was due to his courage that the kingdom was established, its enemies subdued and the way prepared for a period of unprecedented prosperity under his son and successor Solomon.

Wars have proved, if they have proved nothing else, that courage is perhaps the most admired human virtue there is. There are races and even religions where adultery, theft and murder may in certain circumstances be condoned; but cowardice never. People will listen to the wise men, they will try to imitate the good, but it is only the brave, the physically and morally courageous, whom they will follow, come hell or high water.

But it is moral courage that is most important in a leader: the courage to takes risks, to make decisions, and even where necessary to overrule the opinion of others. Deep down inside us all there is the desire to be liked, and one of the first marks of the good leader is that he will not allow himself to be unduly influenced by it. Our politicians may have their faults, but there is one thing I have always admired about men like Wilson, Heath and Thorpe, and that is their courage. They are prepared to be unpopular, to be abused and even loathed by millions of people. I suppose they would not enter Parliament if they were not prepared for this, and we can say that they have only themsleves to blame; but in a sense this sort of courage is required in all who take the lead, whether as chairman of a committee or headmaster of a huge comprehensive school. Brains alone will never make a man a good leader; he must have guts.

But there was another aspect of David's character which we must observe, namely his *sympathy*. It is one thing to make people come after you but another to make them come to you; and that is what David was able to do. He attracted people. Jonathan fell for him and though he knew that David and not he must succeed Saul there was never a shred of resentment nor a vestige of of jealousy.

Later, as a fugitive and exile, it was to him that people turned if they had a grievance or problem. They felt he was a man who understood, who had been through trouble himself. He became the kind of person to whom people unlock the secret recesses of their heart and conscience, a natural confessor.

To some men in a remarkable way this gift is given. 'I could tell him anything' you hear someone say; and you know that he is referring to the kind of person who always has time, who never appears shocked and to whom the act of unburdening in itself, quite apart from any advice that may follow, will be a balm and a relief.

The wise leader 'never appears shocked', not because he is insensitive to sin, or still less because he is blasé, but because the shock is absorbed by his knowledge of human nature. He knows the wickedness of which he himself is capable, and he can therefore listen with sympathy and understanding .'Such tales of woe I have heard in Moody's enquiry room,' wrote Henry Drummond, 'that I've felt I must go and change my clothes after the contact.' But this loathing of sin did not alter the fact that at the age of twenty-three he was trusted and consulted by thousands of his fellow-men.

There is one further quality which David possessed and which we must note, namely his *magnanimity*. It comes out again and again. He refused to take advantage of Saul and slay him by stealth, and on two occasions spared the life of his enemy against the advice of his friends; and when Saul finally fell in battle and David composed his famous lament there is never a hint of vindictiveness or personal triumph. This generosity was extended to Saul's family. He would not take revenge on Saul's son who rebelled against him, and executed those who without authority slew him in his own house; and he sought out and befriended Saul's crippled grandson Mephibosheth. His attitude towards his own spoilt and rebellious son Absalom, while exasperating his advisers and bordering on the sentimental, is just one more example of how bad a hater he was and how ready to believe and hope for the best.

'In war resolution; in defeat defiance; in victory magnanimity; in peace goodwill.' Those are the words which adorn the inside cover of the first volume of Sir Winston Churchill's *War Memoirs*. A study of his own life proves how aptly they apply to himself and this may be one reason why I have often felt there is such an interesting comparison between that great statesman born just 100 years ago, and Judah's greatest king.

We are often reminded of the importance of being a good loser, but the leader must also learn the art of winning. It is very hard sometimes to resist the temptation to boast or to gloat. 'Magnanimity in politics is not seldom the truest wisdom,' said Burke; and not only in politics. The good leader must be ready to applaud what is of value in the argument he has just demolished or the plan he has discarded, to restore with a smile the man he has rebuked, and cover up as best he can for the one who has spoken foolishly or acted wrongly.

But we must not leave this splendid Old Testament leader without referring to his 'epitaph' in the Book of Acts. 'And when God had removed Saul He raised up unto them David to be their king; to whom he gave testimony and said "I have found David the son of Jesse a man after mine own heart who shall fulfil all my will"' (Acts 13: 22).

This was the real crown that King David wore. He was a man after God's own heart. Despite every vicissitude and failure, his heart was always in the right place. His hands strayed, his feet often slipped, but his 'heart was fixed, trusting in the Lord' (Psalm 112: 7). Perverse and foolish oft he strayed, as he was the first to admit; but he really loved the Lord and he returned to Him in penitence and sorrow after every failure.

Beyond economic prosperity and political unity, both of which he achieved, it was his aim and purpose to make his country the centre of true spiritual worship. It was due to him that the ark was recovered and brought back from exile; and he made the plans for the Temple which was finally built by Solomon his son. Historians looked back and realized that 'he served his own generation by the will of God,' and that in spite of all his failures here was the ideal king, the man after God's own heart.

Discussion Points

1. 'A man after My own heart.' That was how God described David (Acts 13: 22). What qualities in David's life especially endeared him to the Lord? (Psalms 23; 27; 51; 121).
2. What do David and Jonathan have to teach us about the value and privilege of Christian friendship? (1 Samuel 18; 19, 2 Samuel 1).
3. Is it possible for a leader to combine the humanity of David with the authority of Moses? Who succeeded in doing so perfectly? (John 1: 14 & 17).
4. 'David was not a particularly good judge of men.' Do you agree with that verdict? What makes someone 'a good judge' in this respect?
5. Should a Christian leader aim to be 'popular'.
6. What practical steps can an aspiring leader, and one who has perhaps earned rapid promotion, take to remain humble?

7. Daniel—The Statesman

'It is no good. We shall never get him impeached in this way. The private detective agency can find no fault with his domestic life, and as we know his official conduct is beyond reproach. There is only one thing left. We must get the King to outlaw the man's religion, and then charge him with treason when he continues to practise it.'

That was how Daniel was trapped, and how King Darius, outmanoeuvred by his cabinet, was forced to commit his prime minister to the den of lions. The rest of the story we know well.

Daniel's courage, moral as well as physical, has become proverbial; but it is not so much of this that we shall think, though it will shine through at every point, but rather how this remarkable man, an exile in an alien country, involved himself in the affairs of that nation without compromise or corruption.

After the fall of Jerusalem, Nebuchadnezzar had chosen several good-looking and well-educated young men of noble birth to take back as prospective courtiers to Babylon. Daniel was among those who underwent the special period of three years' training which was prescribed for them, and the rest of his life, with perhaps one possible period of eclipse under Belshazzar, was spent in the royal service.

In his early days, Daniel probably had no choice in the matter. He was forced willy-nilly into the life of courtier, politician and statesman; but it is likely that towards the end he could have retired quietly had he chosen to do so, but preferred instead to continue to interest himself in what he called 'the king's business'.

It is a popular heresy in some quarters to suppose that a spiritually-minded Christian should play no part in the affairs of local or national government. It is true that he may sometimes answer this sort of call with misgiving and reluctance; but much of the present-day distress in such things as housing, social welfare and industrial relations might have been averted or would have been worse, according to the part played by Christians in Parliament or town hall. As I understand it, one of the main thrusts of the Bishop of Woolwich's important book *Built as a City* is that Christian influence, like salt, must be present in the cooking and not just dabbed on the potatoes from a pile on the side of the plate.

Some years ago I used to sit from time to time on the selection boards which examined candidates for the Christian ministry. One problem that continually faced us was whether, by encouraging a man to be ordained, we would actually be robbing the Church of someone who could render more effective service as a layman. It was sometimes a difficult decision to make, particularly having regard to the time and money involved.

Perhaps the long-term answer will lie in the auxiliary ministry in which men and women can serve without being required to abandon their previous calling. The present system is not flexible enough to meet the needs of modern society, and the gulf between clergy and laity is still too wide and too rigid.

Nevertheless, it is encouraging to know that there are men and women in public life who are bending all their energies in the right direction and doing all they can to apply Christian principles and standards in the fields of legislation and administration.

Such men are faced with temptations of which others know little or nothing. First, they are tempted to compromise, perhaps because they often have to work with others who do not share their ideals and faith. Compromise, of course, can be a good thing if it describes the give-and-take by which people reach agreement when no important principle is at stake; but in the sense we are using it here, it is a bad thing, because it implies the dilution or adulteration of firmly-held beliefs to appease an opponent or for personal advantage.

We find that right from the start Daniel took a clear stand. As a boy he was in the custody of the king's steward, and was expected to eat the food which was enjoyed at the high table. He knew that this food had been offered to heathen idols and so, along with his friends, he asked to be excused. After some hesitation, the steward agreed. Daniel's decision was honoured by God, for the king made no complaint about the effect of the simpler vegetarian diet upon the health or appearance of his royal pages.

The next test came when he was called to interpret the dream of Nebuchadnezzar, and many years later the writing on the wall at Belshazzar's feast. In both cases he could easily have tampered with the truth, and found a favourable interpretation instead of one which involved insanity in the one case and death in the other; but again Daniel refused to compromise. He told the whole unpalatable truth and faced the consequences.

The final and most fearful test came when he refused the king's edict to worship only him, and continued to pray openly and regularly to his God as he had always done. A lesser man would have shut the windows through which he was seen, or chosen a private place; but not Daniel.

Compromise is the great temptation of all who are engaged in secular forms of leadership. It does not arise so much in specifically Christian work where spiritual standards are the rule. It can begin perhaps when a newly-appointed prefect or monitor turns a blind eye on the misdemeanours of the friends over whom he has been promoted and is expected to exercise authority. It can end in Parliament when a member casts his vote in favour of legislation which violates his Christian conscience in order to appease the demands of the party whip.

It is the principle of the double standard, one official and one private, which is so dangerous and has to be guarded against by leaders. Where I went to school there was a clock with two faces, one looking down the drive, the other into what we called the front quad. I was told that before I arrived the two faces told different times, and whether you were early or late for an appointment would depend upon which face you were going by.

Daniel only had one face. There was a consistency about his life—a divine predictability; he always rang true.

> 'I would go stark and let my meanings show
> Clear as a milk white feather in a crow
> Or a black stallion on a field of snow

That describes Daniel, because the public official man was the same as the private domestic man.

The other danger which faces leaders in public life is corruption. There are from time to time tragic examples of this: justice perverted through a bribe; a contract given for a favour shown; even an honour for a fee.

Kipling wrote a devastating little poem entitled *Gehazi* in which he compared the then newly-appointed Lord Chief Justice (who had been involved in unwise financial dealings) with that classic example of corruption in the Old Testament, Gehazi, the servant of Elisha, who muscled in on his master's refusal of a gift, in order to feather his own nest.

> 'Take order now Gehazi
> That no man talk aside
> In secret with his judges
> The while his case is tried.
> Lest he should show them—reason
> To keep the matter hid

And subtly lead the questions
Away from what he did.'

It is probably true to say that men are more easily corrupted by favour than by fear, simply because greed is a commoner sin than cowardice. The man who is unmoved by threats may be persuaded to promote someone who has been generous to him rather than the person who deserves promotion on merit; or to prefer the man who has done him a good turn, or comes from the same school, or is connected by marriage.

There is a phrase in the Book of Common Prayer which modern commentators love to alter. It is where we pray that those in authority may 'truly and indifferently minister justice'. Nowadays we are asked to say 'truly and impartially'. The latter phrase of course conveys an important truth, but not the one originally intended. To minister justice indifferently meant that the judge was indifferent to any effect his judgement might have upon himself, whether it brought him promotion or disfavour; and referred to the practice of interference with the judiciary prevalent in those days.

Daniel eschewed such ideas. Notice the magnificent answer he gave to Belshazzar and which shows what he thought of such conduct. Hoping no doubt for a favourable interpretation of the writing on the wall, the king promises Daniel promotion and wealth. To a man who at that time may have been living in obscurity, retirement or even disfavour, the suggestion must have been attractive, but Daniel replied, 'Your gifts you may keep for yourself; or else give your rewards to another' (Daniel 5: 17). No wonder his fellow-cabinet ministers, mad with jealousy though they were, had to admit that when they 'began to look round for some pretext to attack Daniel's administration of the kingdom . . . . they failed to find any malpractice on his part for he was faithful to his trust' (Daniel 6: 4). Daniel is perhaps the supreme example in the Bible of the man who walked white in a world that was black and sets a pattern for all to follow:

> 'That we like him may walk uncowed
> By fear or favour of the crowd.'

But in closing, let us look at the secrets of Daniel's splendid character. What was the hidden source of his courage and faith? What secret springs of action inspired his behaviour? We know next to nothing about his upbringing, except to say that it was certainly princely and godly; but three things do emerge which help to explain the steadfastness of his later life.

First he was a man of *principle*. Like John the Baptist he was no reed shaken with the wind. Heinrich Mann, in the character of Diederich Hessling, gives us a picture of the exact opposite of Daniel: a weak, vacillating and cowardly creature, to whom right and wrong were not dictated by objective standards but by opportunism bolstered up by obedience to superior orders uncritically accepted. How rightly he called the book *Man of Straw*! Daniel was made of sterner stuff. To him right was right and wrong was wrong. He saw things clearly in black and white, not in the pastel shades of grey and cream.

But we must be clear what we mean by 'principle'. Bernard Shaw in *The Man of Destiny* says, 'There is nothing so good or so bad that you will not find an Englishman doing; but you will never find an Englishman in the wrong. He does everything on principle.' In other words, he tries to justify on moral grounds everything he wants to do, whether good or bad.

This comes from treating our prejudices as if they were principles, and giving them our slavish loyalty. A principle is the response we make to an objective standard; while a prejudice is a subjective judgement or opinion. The wise leader distinguishes between the two, in himself as well as in other people; and while adhering strongly to principles, he will not allow himself to be swayed by prejudice. He must be firm on matters of right and wrong, but flexible on matters of taste.

Secondly Daniel was a man of *habit*. We are told that it was his custom to pray three times a day, a habit he refused to abandon even under threat of death. If principles are the foundations of the building of character, then habits are its scaffolding—the framework which gives cohesion and shape to a man's life. We sometimes speak almost disparagingly of someone as being a 'creature of habit', as though it were an unworthy thing to be; but this is not necessarily so at all. Provided those habits are good ones they help to guarantee that a man's life will develop and mature along the right lines.

Reading the lives of great leaders, military and political, I find it is usually the case that they were men who, quite early in life, developed certain habits. There was a discipline about them. They lived well-ordered lives, regulated by reference to certain fixed points to which they would try to adhere.

A 'habit' is literally something we wear—for example, a 'riding habit'. It is part of us and something by which we are recognized; and the Christian leader must be known, not only for the more spiritual habits of prayer and Bible reading, but also for his scrupulous and businesslike way of life.

I remember, for instance, how meticulous my Bishop used to be in the way he answered letters. I always received full and prompt replies, even when I was a mere curate, often written in his own hand and, I suspect, late at night. In this way alone he commended himself to me as a leader of men, and I have tried to follow his example.

Finally Daniel was fortunate indeed in his *friends*. Shadrach, Meshach and Abed-nego rather faded from the story, but they are there at the beginning, and we know that it was their presence and their prayers that upheld Daniel in the early difficult days of his exile.

I can well remember the enormous help a few Christian friends were to me at boarding school. To talk and pray with them was a great privilege and inspiration. 'Two are better than one; they receive a good reward for their toil, because, if one falls the other can help his companion up again; but alas for the man who falls alone with no partner to help him' (Ecclesiastes 4: 9 and 10).

Leadership in any field can be a lonely occupation. Society is shaped like a pyramid and those at the very top often have few to whom they can turn and confide everything, and with whom they can share responsibility; but those who can be trusted as chosen friends, whose sympathy, counsel and prayers can be counted upon, will help to keep the leader true to himself, to those he leads, and above all to God.

Discussion Points

1. 'A man greatly beloved' (Daniel 10: 11). Can you see why Daniel is referred to in this way? (Daniel 1: 8; 6: 10; Hebrews 11: 33).
2. Daniel was noted for his great wisdom (Daniel 1: 4; 2: 14–30; 12: 3). What is wisdom, and where is it to be found? (James 1: 5, 6; Proverbs 9: 10; 1 Corinthians 1: 30).
3. When is it a good thing to compromise, and when is it a bad thing? Where is the dividing line?
4. 'Hating bribes brings happiness.' (Proverbs 15: 27, Living Bible). How would you apply that advice to a would-be leader?
5. What kind of people should a Christian choose for his friends?
6. Is loneliness bound to be part of the price that you pay for being a leader?

8. John—The Reformer

I have always enjoyed studying the lives of what might be called 'Great Second Strings'—leaders, that is to say, who have never quite reached the top; men and women who prepared the way for others to take the limelight; the pace-makers or silver medallists.

As a boy in the 1920s and '30s I was a keen follower of county cricket, and I can still remember the aura which surrounded that great pair of opening batsmen—Hobbs and Sutcliffe. Measured by their results, there was not a great deal to choose between them; but it would have been as unthinkable to have referred to them as 'Sutcliffe and Hobbs' as to speak of 'Kidney and Steak', for Hobbs was always the dominant and Sutcliffe the recessive partner in the firm.

We often find the same sort of thing in entertainment and politics. Take music, for example. People will remember Gerald Moore not so much as an extremely accomplished pianist (which he certainly was) but as the accompanist of even greater virtuosos: while in politics Lord Butler has been aptly described as the 'best Prime Minister we never had'.

When we turn to the Bible, we find that its pages abound with the names of men who were famous because they were associated with even more important personalities: Aaron, Caleb, Jonathan, Barnabas, Silas and—perhaps the greatest of them all—John the Baptist. He deserves a special place in the hearts of those who never quite reach the top—the second in command, the assistant manager, the deputy head, the vice captain. He is in fact the patron saint of silver medallists.

John might have made a great name for himself, but his true greatness consisted in the unique and historical way he played the part of 'Best Man' to Jesus; and he sought nothing higher for himself than in due course to give way to him as the moon at daybreak gives way to the sun. 'He must increase, but I must decrease' (John 3: 30) was the motto he lived up to all through his life.

In this sense, John was not so much a leader as an indicator. He pointed men and women away from himself towards Christ. 'Behold the Lamb of God' (John 1: 29), he cried as he stretched out his hand towards the one who, although he came after him in time, was before him in precedence.

This, of course, is part of the vocation of all Christians, whether leaders or not, to point people to Christ; but in John's case it took place literally and in a historical context. Men heard him speak and they followed Jesus. His congregation began to dwindle while that of Jesus swelled. Jesus' name began to replace his on the hoardings and in the headlines. Gounod, the composer, tells us that, as a young man he used to talk a great deal about himself, his achievements and ambitions. Then it became 'I and Mozart', a little later 'Mozart and I', and finally just 'Mozart'. It was like that with John, and what made him great was that he was willing for it to happen.

Two interesting metaphors are used to describe John. He called himself a voice (Mark 1: 3); but a voice tells us very little unless it utters a word. Only then does it become significant and meaningful, and Jesus was that Word (John 1: 14) which expressed itself through the voice. Again John was a lamp (John 5: 35 N.E.B.); but a lamp by itself is of no use. It is just a meaningless ornament until the light shines through it; and Jesus was that light, 'the light of the world' (John 8: 12), using human lives to reflect and magnify his rays. To change the metaphor, we might say that Jesus was the painting that men came to see and admire, while John was merely the frame.

In one place Paul refers to himself as being 'nothing' (2 Corinthians 12: 11). John the Baptist would have echoed that thought. He regarded himself simply as the figure '0', and the significance and latent value of that figure is only discovered when you put it after the figure 1. John was humble enough to realize that apart from Christ he could do and in fact was precisely nothing.

From this position, John exercised a tremendous influence upon the moral, social and spiritual life of his country. In the best sense of the word, he was a radical, hacking at the very roots of personal and national conduct (Luke 3). No one escaped his 'axe'. The religious leaders were charged with hypocrisy. The common people were made to see their greed, the tax collectors their dishonesty, and the soldiers were warned against bullying, blackmail and discontent. Even Herod himself did not escape censure as John accused him of immorality. Fearlessly he cleared a pathway through this jungle of corruption, a pathway of national repentance along which the gospel could march unimpeded. High and low, rich and poor, all came under the life-giving influence of his teaching, until finally the voice was silenced and the lamp broken.

It is worth considering carefully the difference between influence and power, because although John never wielded the sort of power which came to men like Joseph and Moses, his influence was profound and lasting. We might say that power is the influence which a man owes chiefly to his position, while influence is the power he owes to his character. It follows that influence often works in a quieter, more personal and pervasive way, perhaps at a deeper level than power, and sometimes most effectively behind the scenes. We might compare it to the quiet strength of a river rather than the mighty force of the sea.

'A noise like of a hidden brook in the leafy month of
    June
That to the sleeping woods all night singeth a quiet
    tune.'

At one stage in his life George Whitefield, the great
eighteenth-century evangelist, exercised a marvellous
influence for good upon quite a wide circle of landed
gentry and noblemen. Some responded eagerly to his
message, but others resisted and did their best to urge
King George II to restrain him. The King jokingly
replied, 'I believe the best way will be to make a bishop
of him'. He realized that in this way Whitefield would
exchange a national and unrestricted influence for local
and limited power: and more subtly, he may have seen
something of the corrupting effect of that power on
contemporary members of the episcopal bench, an effect
which even Whitefield might have found it hard to escape.

Needless to say, nothing came of the idea and George
Whitefield was probably very happy to be spared such a
fate, and continued for some years to turn the hearts of
people to God in this country and in North America. He
refused to exchange influence for power. And it may be for
this same reason that a man I know, in a position of
very great influence, has, according to reliable news-
paper reports, refused at least two bishoprics.

Another example was Professor Henry Drummond,
who 100 years ago did such a deep and lasting spiritual
work amongst Scottish students. There came a point in
his career when he was urged by Gladstone to stand for
Parliament, but he knew that he could only achieve
greater power by abandoning the personal influence he
was exercising, and 'that by walking in the fixed walk of
life' that had been assigned to him as he felt by God, he
could 'do more for every cause of truth and righteousness'.

It would be quite wrong to infer from what has just
been said that when a man becomes a public figure in

church or state he is thereby choosing a second-best course. Far from it. The more outstanding Christians there are in such positions, the better for the cause of Christ. But anyone invited to fill a prominent office must ask himself whether, by accepting the power it brings, he is going to limit the influence 'for truth and righteousness' which he could otherwise exercise privately over people and perhaps events.

It was in the 'walk of life' that God had assigned to him that John the Baptist occupied himself so fully and effectively. It was not simply that he bore no grudge at being overtaken by a younger man who was also a relative, but he resented and fiercely repudiated any suggestion that he should occupy a more prominent position for himself. When reporters wanted to know who he was, and whether he himself was the long-expected Messiah, his answers got shorter and sharper. 'I am not the Christ', 'I am not', and finally 'No' (John 1: 19–21).

We must not think of John as a sort of *éminence grise*, the sinister power behind the throne into whose hands all the strings ultimately find their way and are manipulated according to his will. Not at all, intrigue of any sort was completely foreign to his nature, for there was nothing devious or disingenuous about John the Baptist.

This is perhaps an apt moment to consider the question of promotion and the Christian's attitude towards it. Generally speaking, promotion is of two kinds—automatic and selective. Automatic promotion is something which most people have a right to expect until about half way through their working life. The soldier, the teacher, the businessman, unless he blots his copy book pretty badly, will travel up a fairly well-worn escalator or career structure.

But then perhaps in early middle life the field begins to thin out and the real race is on. Some drop out at this stage, either because they are unqualified or because they lack the necessary competitive spirit to get to the top, and prefer a quiet life to an important one. But for those who remain there are now fewer jobs than candidates and the sides of the pyramid seem to get steeper.

What principles should guide the Christian at this stage? He is naturally and rightly ambitious and wants to succeed. He feels, we will suppose, that promotion will increase his influence as well as his income. Does he start dropping hints, putting out feelers, pulling strings? Or does he just sit back and wait upon events?

The spiritual man will, I think, be guided chiefly by two things. First, he will certainly not entertain the idea of place-seeking and wire-pulling. He will remember the command of the Lord 'Seekest thou great things for thyself? Seek them not' (Jeremiah 45: 5). Secondly, he will remember that 'promotion cometh neither from the east nor from the west nor from the south. But God is judge: He putteth down one and setteth up another' (Psalm 75: 6 and 7). In other words, after taking the normal sensible steps of form-filling, getting referees and making application, he is content to leave the result with God, believing that He can control the outcome and that His will will be done. He will not therefore be unduly elated at success or depressed by failure, because he has not made promotion an indispensable prize at which to grasp, and whatever the result may be he can trace the hand of God.

John's humility showed itself in another attractive way. He was quite unspoiled by success, and make no mistake, he was astoundingly successful. This rough-cut, untrained preacher drew enormous congregations for 'they flocked to him from Jerusalem, from all Judaea and the whole Jordan valley' (Matthew 3: 5 N.E.B.). Every clergyman knows that feeling of elation and even excitement as he sees his congregation filling up, and at times he has to resist the temptation to intercept the credit which should go to God, or to respond to flattery, or to adjust his message to make it more palatable to 'Sir Luke Warm' who is putting in one of his rare appearances at church.

In fact, John might have done quite well for himself, had he chosen to, for it was not just the common people who enjoyed his sermons, but we are told that Herod also 'liked to listen to him' (Mark 6:20 N.E.B.). But he refused to dilute his message to suit people, and he insisted on the simple, austere way of life which he had chosen from the start.

What would John the Baptist have had to say about the 'standard of living' of which we hear so much today, and the fact that we seem to demand as a right that it should steadily improve year by year, so that the luxuries of yesterday become the necessities of today? He was made of sterner stuff, and the comment of Jesus is interesting, 'What went you out into the wilderness to see . . . a man clothed in soft raiment? Behold, they that wear soft clothing are in kings' houses' (Luke 7:25). John preferred his coat of camels' hair and his diet of locusts and wild honey which, incidentally, and according to Dr. Livingstone, was both palatable and nourishing.

Perhaps not many are called to deprive themselves so completely of the good things of life as John was, and Jesus, as we know, while he applauded him, did not follow John in this respect. But is there a danger, even amongst keen Christians, of demanding as a right what our fathers accepted as a privilege? Has the note of personal sacrifice been muted too much in the materialistic progress of the last twenty-five years. Two friends of mine wrote to me the other day about a matter which was greatly worrying them, and told me that they were going to take an early opportunity of having a day of prayer and fasting in order to lay their problem before the Lord. I felt ashamed to realize that this was something I had never done myself.

I have television, black and white, and have had it for many years. Sometimes on special occasions, such as a royal wedding, I am invited by friends to watch their coloured television, and of course there is no comparison between the two. But when the time comes for me to get another set will I, I wonder, have the strength of will to get black and white, or has colour ceased to be a luxury and become a necessity?

And what about girl friends and boy friends? I was talking recently to two Christian students and they were telling me what a distraction an absorbing friendship with a member of the opposite sex can be at a time when academic study ought to be taking most of their energy and attention. It was only after a little while, they said that they realized how foolish is the idea that a girl friend or a boy friend is a necessary status symbol in college life.

Take marriage. How many young people ever seriously ask themselves whether it could possibly be God's will for them to remain single for the kingdom of heaven's sake, or at least to defer marriage until they are clear what God's life-purpose is for them? Of course, in nine cases out of ten it is right and proper, but is there a danger of assuming this a little too easily, of falling in love first and then deciding that it is God's will to marry, rather than the other way round.

For many years I was a chaplain to Dr. Christopher Chavasse, formerly Bishop of Rochester, and he became in some ways like a father to me. I always remember one luncheon party many years ago at Bishopscourt. There was some good-natured and friendly banter and leg-pulling of one or two people who had reached the age of about forty without marrying. Then, as the party broke up, the Bishop turned to one of them and I heard him say 'I never read the passage about remaining a eunuch for the kingdom of heaven's sake without thinking of you.'

I always remember the impact which Howard Guinness's little book *Sacrifice* made when it first hit the student world in the 1930s. It touched on just the sort of things I have been mentioning—the danger of Christians allowing themselves to be swept along by the tide of material progress, and to take it for granted that they must necessarily share in the kind of expensive hobbies and holidays which are available today. 'It is not what you want—it is what you can do without'—I think that was the most helpful thing my old sixth form master ever said to me. I only wish I had heeded it more.

But I think it is only fair to add that there do appear to be signs of a reaction from the blatant materialism of the Sixties. I am amazed, for example, at the generosity of many young people, their sense of service, their care for those in need, and their increasing awareness that 'a man's life consisteth not in the abundance of the things which he possesseth' (Luke 12: 15). It could well be that the tide has turned, and that the young people of today are going to lead us back into paths of simplicity and sacrifice.

But we have seen enough of John to realize that his austerity and humility were anything but negative virtues. He combined them with great authority. Like Moses before him, he taught the 'lamb' of humility to lie down with the 'lion' of authority, but he did it without arming the lamb or taming the lion.

In his book *Orthodoxy*, G. K. Chesterton explains how Christians solve the problem of balance (what Aristotle called 'meson') in personal behaviour. Paganism declared that virtue lay in a compromise between opposing passions; Christianity in their collision. Paganism advocated a mixture of, say, anger and sympathy, or humility and authority; Christianity insisted on keeping them apart, not tempering one with the other but using each to the full as the occasion demanded—red or blue as the situation required but never purple.

We see the perfect examply of this in the life of Jesus himself, where meekness and majesty dwelt in complete harmony; and we see it in John the Baptist, who one moment could thunder forth his denunciation of sin, and the next declare himself unworthy even to lace the sandals of Jesus. Perhaps the secret lies in the fact that the man who is humble before God is exalted before men (1 Peter 5: 6). It was because there was such humility in John's heart that there was such authority in his voice. Certainly in my own experience it has often been the humblest men who have spoken with the greatest authority. They have made so much of God because they have made so little of themselves.

Discussion Points

1. In what practical ways can we point people to Christ in everyday life? (Acts 4: 13; Matthew 5: 16; 1 Thessalonians 1: 6–9; 1 Peter 2: 9).
2. Why is humility such an important virtue? (Matthew 11: 28–30; Psalm 25: 9; James 4: 6–10; Psalm 138: 6; Matthew 18: 1–6).
3. When an offer of promotion comes, what should influence our decision to accept or refuse it?
4. What does 'sacrifice' mean in the context of the ordinary, comfortably-placed Christian in this country today?
5. As far as we know, John did not marry. In what circumstances might a Christian feel it right to remain single?
6. How can we be humble without being 'wet'?

9. Simon Peter—The Working Man

I always like to remember that Jesus was a carpenter or cabinet-maker, as we would probably call him today, and that much of his early life had been spent with saw and plane and hammer. How often he must have looked at some unpromising length of timber as it was brought into his shop and wondered what he could make of it! No doubt with the eye of a creative artist he would see in that wood a desk, table or chair, just as Michaelangelo saw his great masterpiece the statue of David hidden in that huge block of marble at Florence.

And when Jesus stopped working on wood and began on men and women, the habit continued. In a disreputable tax-collector he saw the writer of the first gospel. In the fiery brothers James and John, he saw the future front line soldiers of his church, and in Simon the man of straw he saw Peter the man of rock. Looking at him and into him as they met for the first time, he said 'Thou art Simon . . . thou shalt be called Peter' (John 1: 42).

Simon Peter, perhaps more than any of the others we have studied, was 'made great'. The finished product bore little resemblance to the raw material. Joseph, Daniel, David all gave early promise of what with God's help they would eventually become; in Simon Peter we see rather what he would have been without that help. He was a monument to the grace of God.

But what sort of a man was Simon in the gospel story? First of all, he was proud. We have clear evidence of this in his pushful, impulsive attitude towards people and situations; and we see it especially in his boastful assertion that though all men might forsake his Master he would never do so, but would remain steadfast and true to the end. He was supremely self-confident, sublimely cocksure.

He was also hot-tempered and undisciplined, acting on impulse rather than reason. For example, he leapt rashly and wildly to the help of Jesus at the time of his arrest, slashing at the high priest's servant. Happily he was such a bad shot that he only sliced off the man's ear, and Jesus was able to put that right, but it might have been very much more serious.

But he not only suffered from a hot head. He also had cold feet; for when the supreme test came, and he was called upon to stand up for Jesus, he completely lost his nerve and was routed by one of the palace waitresses.

Poor Simon! No wonder we read that 'he went out and wept bitterly' (Matthew 26: 75). But those tears were the best thing that could possibly have happened. They marked the turning point, literally the watershed of his life; and slowly from that miserable and disastrous lowest point he began the long road of recovery. It would hardly have been possible to have described anyone less like a leader than Simon Peter at this stage; for a man lacking humility, self-control and courage would be rejected as a candidate for any job where personal responsibility was required.

But let us turn that photograph with its face to the wall for a moment and look at another much more promising one, this time of Peter in the Acts.

We notice, first of all, a look of humility. From the day of Pentecost onwards he met with the most staggering success. Hundreds flocked to hear him. New mysterious powers flowed through him. Nothing could halt his advance. The head of a lesser man would have been turned, but in Peter's case there is never a hint of pride, not the merest smudge of conceit. All the credit was given to God, and this man, to use his own words, was 'clothed with humility' (1 Peter 5: 6).

The temper, too, was at last tamed and under proper control. Instead of flying at his opponents, splitting the air with the kind of oaths he probably used when the nets broke, he reasoned firmly and quietly. He had learned to 'be sober and vigilant', as he later told people to whom he wrote one of his letters (1 Peter 5: 8).

And what about the cowardice? That, too, had been conquered. As we know, he was arrested, thrown into prison, and told that the next day he was to be executed. How would you spend what you knew to be your last night? How would I? We do not find Peter, as we might have expected, picking at the locks or tearing at the bars of his cell. We find him instead asleep between his gaolers, just as calm and composed as his Master had been during that storm-tossed voyage on Lake Galilee. To use his own words once again, he had learnt to cast all his cares upon the Lord who cared for him (1 Peter 5: 7). What accounts for the change? What made the difference? What mysterious alchemy had been at work, turning lead into gold, straw into steel, sand into stone?

In a word, it was due to what has been called 'the transforming friendship of Christ'. Sometimes we say of someone we know well that 'he is a new person'. We mean that an operation, perhaps, or a holiday, or marriage has completely transformed him. Whereas he was listless, morose and disintegrated, now he has a new strength and sense of purpose.

That is what happened to Simon Peter. In finding Christ, he found himself. Jesus became the one great integrating force in his life, drawing together every side of his personality. 'In Christ' he had become 'a new creature' (2 Corinthians 5: 17).

I find this immensely encouraging. It shows us that we can never write anyone off, because there is no limit to the power of Christ to change people's lives. He can humble the proud, tame the wild and make the coward brave. There is a sense in which no one is really 'himself' until he is 'in Christ'; for we do not know what is in that person until Christ has brought it out.

It reminds me too that I need never despair, and that I can believe in the recoverability of man at his worst; for He is able to save to the 'guttermost' all who come to Him (Hebrews 7: 25). If He can turn that deceitful pretender Jacob into a spiritual prince, and if He can work the same sort of miracle in Simon Peter, is there anyone beyond His reach? Is there anyone whom the God of Jacob and of Simon cannot transform?

Sometimes I meet people who are Christian leaders today, and I look back over ten or twenty years and marvel at what God has done for them. I marvel, too, at my own lack of faith all those years ago in supposing that nothing could reach them.

But let us look more closely at the personal relations which existed and developed between Peter and Jesus in this 'transforming friendship'. On at least three occasions, they talked together alone and each time Simon Peter made an important discovery and took a vital step forward. The first occasion was after that miraculous haul of fishes on the lake when, overcome with a sense of shame, he fell at Jesus' feet and said 'Depart from me for I am a sinful man, O Lord' (Luke 5: 8). He saw himself for the first time, perhaps, as the sinner he really was.

The second occasion was at Caesarea Philippi, when he was given that insight to see Jesus as He was—'Thou art the Christ, the Son of the Living God' (Matthew 16: 16)— and this was followed and confirmed by the vision on the Mount of Transfiguration. From that point onwards, Jesus was not just the Son of man but something infinitely more wonderful.

'If Jesus Christ be man and only a man! I say,
Him will I love and serve and to him will I cleave alway.

But if Jesus Christ be God, and the Son of God, I
  swear
I will follow Him through earth, through water, fire
  and air.'

The third occasion was after the resurrection when, in
response to his repeated profession of love, Jesus
showed him what was to be his form of service and
just where it would lead (John 21).

The fuse that was laid at the lakeside was lit on the
mountain and finally exploded on that early morning
walk. Simon had become Peter.

It is interesting to notice, too, that after each interview,
Simon was given as it were a Certificate of Service.
'From henceforth you shall catch men.' 'I will give you
the keys of the Kingdom.' 'Feed my sheep.' He was to
be a fisherman, a porter or door-keeper and a shepherd.
He was.to win people for Christ, to unlock the mysteries
of the Kingdom to them and to nourish and care for
them as a shepherd.

Simon Peter is an 'Everyman', that it to say one with
whom all of us can easily identify ourselves. His life is
not so much a photograph as a mirror, and as we look
at it we do not find ourselves saying 'Poor Peter' but
rather 'Poor me'.

He shows us leadership in its simplest, most direct
and spiritual form—one in which all men and women as
uneducated as he himself was—can take part: the leading
of people to Christ.

This book may be read by some who feel that they
lack, and can never hope to acquire, the outstanding
qualities of Joseph, Moses or Paul. We cannot, it is true,
all be Pauls, but perhaps we can all be Peters. We can
work by hook, by key and crook. We can be fishers,
porters or shepherds, and in fulfilling this work we are
exercising leadership of a most valuable and important
kind.

We need the hook. There are those in our office or home or street who, but for us, may never have the chance to hear about Christ. Is there a service or meeting to which we can invite them? A house group? Is there a book we can lend or a testimony that we can give?

Then we shall need a key. There are many who are puzzled about the true meaning of the Christian faith and it is our duty and privilege to explain things to them; to give, as Peter himself insisted, a reason for the hope that is in us (1 Peter 3: 15). This means study on our part and a careful attempt to grapple with and master the mystery of our faith.

And we shall need the crook. The instrument the shepherd uses for guiding and guarding those who have come to Christ. They must be drawn into the fellowship of other Christians, welcomed and made to feel at home. They must be helped to adjust themselves at home and at work in an environment which is probably hostile and certainly indifferent to their new-found faith. They must be furnished with the aids to Christian living in the shape of books, Bible-reading notes and opportunities for service.

* * *

When the final tale is told and the score is added up, I have a feeling that it may be some of these unsung leaders who, through personal contact with others, will be found to have achieved most. To them it may never be given 'to read their history in a nation's eyes' but many will remember them as an 'ornament of their times' and thank God on their behalf.

Such men and women deserve to take their place among the greater and more obvious leaders we have been considering. For leadership, unless in the long term it brings people face to face with Christ is, from the Christian point of view, meaningless and wasted; and those who may never aspire to the great offices that some men are called to occupy, may in a quiet and humble way do a work of even greater and more lasting value.

I can think of one such as I write, to whom more than to anyone else I owe my own conversion to Christ more than 40 years ago. He was not endowed with some of the outward qualities of leadership we have been considering. He never hit the headlines or sought publicity. He never made a name for himself, but in the field of quiet personal communication of the gospel he was probably unsurpassed in his generation, and I never think of him without being reminded of Daniel's famous prophecy that 'they that be wise shall shine as the brightness of the firmament; and they that turn many to righteousness as the stars for ever and ever' (Daniel 12: 3).

But successful leadership in these fields will depend for us, as it did for Simon Peter, upon that personal relationship with the Lord. He must touch the conscience, convicting us of sin and offering forgiveness. He must enlighten the mind so that we realize that He is no mere man, but the Son of God. He must warm the heart so that we are willing and ready to spend and be spent in His service—'To give and not to count the cost, to fight and not to heed the wounds, to toil and not to seek for rest.'

Perhaps one reason why our Christian leadership may be less effective and convincing than it should be is that we do not have regular interviews with the Lord when these matters can be checked and if necessary put right. The conscience is allowed to become insensitive, the mind clouded by doubt, and the heart cold. We need another visit to the mountain, another walk by the sea shore. These interviews are not just 'once for all'. We need regular and frequent servicing if the spiritual glow is to be kept bright enough for others to see and to follow.

Discussion Points

1. Reading 1 Peter 5, what vital lessons is it apparent that Peter had learnt since first meeting Jesus?
2. What 'tools' does Jesus the 'Carpenter' sometimes use to mend, shape and beautify our lives? (See 1 Peter 1: 6, 7; 2: 20–21; 3: 17; 4: 12–16; 5: 8–10; 2 Peter 1: 5–8).
3. 'Pride goes before a fall.' This was true of Peter, but can you think of everyday examples of how it could apply to us?
4. What makes a good 'fisherman' (Matthew 4: 19) and a good 'shepherd' (John 21)?
5. How and why is it that God so often uses 'unlearned and ignorant men' (Acts 4: 13) to do His work? Can you think of other examples in the Bible?
6. When someone becomes a Christian, how does it affect the gifts, talents and qualities which he possessed before? And how is his temperament affected?

10. Paul—The Missionary Explorer

It is interesting to reflect how many great leaders have spent a good part of their lives in exile or in prison. Again and again in this century, for instance, a man has been released from captivity or brought back from exile to assume supreme authority in his native land. We think at once of DeValera, Makarios, Kenyatta and others.

And of all the leaders we have been considering, only Joshua and Samuel escaped this sort of experience. Moses and David knew what it was to be a fugitive; Joseph, Daniel, John the Baptist, Peter, Samson and Paul all knew prison from the inside, even though Daniel's incarceration, surely the most terrifying of them all, only lasted for one night.

But few experienced quite the loneliness and deprivation which came to Paul. At least four years were spent in some form of confinement, ending with his death under the Emperor Nero; and prison may have been almost a welcome relief from the beatings, stonings, shipwrecks and perils which formed the perpetual accompaniment of his missionary life.

'Yes, without cheer of sister or of daughter,
 Yes, without stay of father or of son;
 Lone on the land and homeless in the water
 Pass I in patience till the work be done.'

But what can anyone say about Paul that has not been said a hundred times before and very much better? And how can we begin to take the measure of this remarkable man, incomparably the greatest Christian leader there has ever been?

For more than thirty years he worked incessantly, travelling, preaching, visiting and writing. At the end of that time, the Gospel had spread from Jerusalem through Asia Minor into Greece and Italy and even as far westwards as Spain; while in many of the most important centres of trade and commerce such as Ephesus, Corinth and Rome, a Christian community had become established; and all this under God was due to the vision, self-sacrifice and courage of this unique Christian.

We might write at length of Paul the saint for, in the truest sense of that word, none ever deserved the title more than he. Like John the Baptist, he spoke and wrote with great authority yet he was a man of the deepest humility. He could rebuke, but he did so in love. He could be angry, but he could also shed tears of sympathy and sorrow. He suffered an appalling catalogue of misfortune, but he never wavered or weakened and to the very end every word he spoke or wrote breathed out his care for the Christian churches.

Or what about Paul the pastor? What did the members of these individual churches think of their leader? We get some idea perhaps of what he meant to them by the very moving farewell he took of the elders at Miletus (Acts 20). He prayed for them regularly. He visited them when he could, sparing no pains and accepting every kind of privation. He cared for them spiritually and physically, spending and being spent in their service. He wrote to them. He preached for them. He died for them.

But there was nothing sentimental about Paul. Some of his letters were sharp and even caused misunderstanding, because his standards were so high. Like every good leader, he made great demands upon his followers and they responded, not from fear or favour, but because they knew that he asked nothing of others that he was not prepared to give himself.

These are aspects of Paul's life and work which could be developed indefinitely, but it is in two rather different ways that we shall consider his particular gifts as a leader. First he was a *strategist*. He worked to a plan. While he lived in the daily hope of the Lord's return, he worked on the assumption that he had a reasonable expectation of life, and planned accordingly. We find in his letters the frequent occurrence of words like 'after' and 'when', referring to the arrangements he was making for future tours and visits. There was nothing haphazard about the way he worked. He knew that there were vital urban centres from which the Gospel would filter to outlying towns and villages, and he was determined to use these as stepping stones across the ancient world.

We have an interesting illustration of this in Acts 16, where we read that Paul and his companions 'tried to go into Bithynia: but the Spirit did not alllow them'. Why were they not allowed to go into Bithynia and what would have happened if they had? Bithynia is the northern part of what we now call Turkey, at that time a rough undeveloped country bordering the Black Sea. There were no doubt precious souls there and valuable work to be done, but for the purpose for which God had called Paul it was a spiritual and strategic backwater. Instead of Bithynia, therefore, Paul was beckoned on towards the thriving cities of Asia Minor and Greece. He knew that by concentrating on Philippi and Corinth he was leaving vast areas unevangelised; but he also knew that, by sowing the seed in these strategic centres, he was giving it the best possible chance to take root and to spread throughout the civilized world. He was working on the well-known principle 'Urbi et orbi'—to the city and to the world. How true are those words in Proverbs 11: 14—'For want of skilful strategy an army is lost; victory is the fruit of long planning.'

Paul's policy served to set a pattern for all missionary endeavour ever since—namely, where possible to work from the centre outwards. There is nothing invidious in making our primary target the key places, people or professions if, in this way, we can reach the largest number of people in the long run.

I remember when I was at school there was one boy who for some reason had the ability to make others follow him. He was not particularly clever or good at games, but I felt that if he were won for Christ, much of the hostility towards the Christian group which at that time existed would evaporate. It happened and the effect was immediate. A new atmosphere prevailed and for the time being the 'enemy' was silenced.

Honesty compels me to admit that it did not last. This particular boy, later to be killed in the war, never really became established as a Christian and rather faded out, but it lasted long enough for me to realize that, other things being equal, it is a sound principle to go for the sort of person who is most likely to influence others. If you want to spread measles, give it to a good mixer; and while the analogy may not be very apt, Christianity has one thing in common with measles—it is caught rather than taught.

The second thing about Paul which made him such an exceptional leader was that he became a perfect *tactician*. Not only did he have an eye for the grand design, but also for the details, and this skill as a tactician is most noticeable in his remarkable gift of self-adaptation.

It is interesting to see in a man of such firmness of character such an astonishing degree of flexibility. He was a man of conviction if ever there was one; but wonderfully adaptable in his approach to situations and people. He was a dogmatist, but also a pragmatist.

Now this quality—the ability to combine these particular opposites—is one of the supreme marks of leadership. To know instinctively when to resist and when to yield; when to abandon a cherished tradition and when to hold fast that which is good; when to forsake one method for another one which perhaps has never been put to the test.

Of course, Paul had certain natural advantages. He was a carefully nurtured Jew who had enjoyed a Greek education and possessed the coveted privilege of Roman citizenship. He combined within his personality the three main cultures of his day and this certainly helped to make his self-adaption easy and natural. There was no grinding of gears, the transmission was automatic and even his worst enemies could never accuse him of hypocrisy. He never adopted a pose, but merely presented the side of his character that had most in common with the people he was with at the time.

This flexibility is a most important quality for a leader to cultivate but how can we do so without becoming inconsistent and chameleon-like? How can the clergyman, for example, appeal equally to the Tory and Labour members of his congregation? the young and the old? the educated and the uneducated? the young convert and the experienced church member?

First of all, we must I think be quite clear exactly what we mean by consistency. Emerson has said that 'a foolish consistency is the hobgoblin of little minds', and Sir Winston Churchill has some interesting things to say on this subject. Writing about political inconsistency he says this, 'A distinction should be drawn at the outset between two kinds of political inconsistency. First, a statesman in contact with the moving current of events, and anxious to keep the ship on an even keel and a steady course, may lean all his weight now on one side and now on the other. His arguments in each case, when contrasted, can be shown to be not only very different in character but contradictory in spirit and opposite in direction. Yet his object will throughout have remained the same. His resolves, his wishes, his outlook may have been unchanged. His methods may be verbally irreconcilable. We cannot call this inconsistency. In fact it may be claimed to be the truest consistency. The only way a man can remain consistent amid changing circumstances is to change with them, while preserving the same dominating purpose.'

We can apply this to the subject of spiritual or moral consistency, and say that the important thing is always to draw the line between a basic principle and a temporary expedient. On more than one occasion, for example, Paul did things which some may have felt to be inconsistent with his Christian profession. For instance, he took a vow, and paid the expenses of four other people to do the same, and although to him it was an outworn and meaningless ritual, to have acted otherwise would have caused unnecessary offence; and so 'to the Jews he became a Jew' (1 Corinthians 9: 22).

He was equally careful in another direction. Some young Christians felt conscience-stricken at the idea of eating meat which, after it had been offered to idols, was sold off cheaply. To Paul idols were empty and meaningless and he could see no harm at all in eating such meat, but if by doing so he offended the conscience of less mature fellow Christians then he would certainly refrain; for 'to the weak he became weak'.

Inconsistent? Yes, but only superficially so, and in fact merely an example of 'the truest consistency'. That inspired Christian writer Oswald Chambers once said this: 'Beware of making a fetish of consistency to your convictions instead of being devoted to God.'

The Christian leader is constantly faced with the need to exercise this sort of tactical discretion. It will be his aim never to ride rough-shod over the scruples and prejudices of his followers, and to do all he can to avoid giving unnecessary offence. If he is staying with those whose custom it is to go to Holy Communion every Sunday, he will join them, even though his own practice may be different. If he is entertaining others, he will be careful to consider their particular tastes, even if they do not coincide with his own. He will try to cultivate Paul's loving sensitivity towards others which seemed to be even more conscious of their feelings than of his own.

This power of self-adaptation also showed itself in all his personal relationships. He had none of Simon Peter's difficulty in this respect. Class, colour and race meant nothing to Paul. He was always on easy terms with the Roman officers, and to authority he showed just the right amount of deference, respectful, but never obsequious. In that little gem of a letter which he wrote to Philemon about a runaway slave, we find that he is equally at home conversing with the master as he is with the servant.

In this country today, there are developing, particularly in the big cities, social and racial groups with their own distinctive cultural and ethnical character. We are, in fact, faced with what almost amounts to a form of neo-tribalism, and those who hope to gain the confidence of people in these groups must be flexible enough to study, understand and even adopt the way of life that is practised among them. As the prophet Ezekiel found (Ezekiel 3: 1–15), this form of self-adaptation can be even more difficult than serving God in a foreign country.

This particular quality of Christian leadership also shows itself in another way, because the one who has it is able to combine under his command men and women of different outlook and temperament. Paul possessed this gift, but of course no one had it to a higher degree than Jesus Himself, as we see from the way in which He chose and then united twelve such very different men as His disciples.

Finally, we see how adaptable Paul was in the presentation of his message. To the Athenians, for example, his approach was quite different from the one he adopted when his congregation was mainly composed of Jews.

He chose for his starting point the presence of an idol with the inscription 'To the unknown God' (Acts 17: 22–31), and he sought to show them from this 'text' that the living God as revealed in Christ was the one whom they ignorantly worshipped and blindly sought.

To adapt the Gospel is not to alter it. Paul was perfectly clear on this point (Galatians 1: 6–9). It means rather to shape the beginning of the Gospel to suit the particular background of the hearers, choosing that aspect of it which is most likely to claim their attention and hold their interest. The age, culture and intelligence of the congregation must determine the starting point we choose, though, of course, never the point at which we finish—personal committal to Christ.

It is noticeable today that the preacher cannot take for granted some of the things he could assume twenty or thirty years ago. The existence of absolute moral standards and objective truth, for example, are challenged as never before; and the preacher must take greater trouble than was once necessary to reinforce and apply these facts.

The wise leader, therefore, will bear this in mind, whether he is speaking himself or training others to do the same. Nothing can alter the substance of the Gospel, but the shape must vary from one generation to another and even from one year to the next; but a loaf of bread is still a loaf whether it is round or rectangular.

I have often found that the difference between a talk for children and one for adults lies not in its substance nor even its basic structure, but solely in its presentation. What 'makes' a 'Children's Talk' is not the presence or absence of certain doctrinal truths, but the length, the language, the tone and the choice of illustrations with which it is presented. In fact, I would even say that is sometimes easier to get across fundamental truths to children than to adults, because one can use pictures (verbal or literal) which one hesitates to use when the audience is composed of sophisticated grown-ups.

I always remember an occasion when I was at Cambridge before the war. I invited a number of students from overseas to a coffee party and Dr. Howard Guinness, a widely-travelled missionary, to speak to them. The talk he gave was one of the finest I have ever heard, because he understood instinctively the culture and background from which his audience came. It appeared that he had visited almost every country represented in the room, and he was listened to with the greatest possible attention.

To write about Paul is, as someone has said, rather like trying to write the history of a fragrance. Everything the Christian leader needs to equip him for his task is to be found in that man's remarkably rounded character and personality. But perhaps it has been of value to stress these two things, strategy and tactics, because they are those which I believe make him almost unique among the spiritual giants whom we have been considering in this book.

Discussion Points

1. What names did Paul choose for himself as a servant of Christ, and what do they teach us about his life and work? (Ephesians 3: 7, 8,; 4: 1; 1:1; 6: 20). Can you find any others in the New Testament?
2. What qualities of Christian leadership can you find in Acts 20: 17–38? And how would apply them today?
3. How do you see yourself, at home or in your work, as a Christian strategist?
4. How far can we adapt ourselves to the feelings and wishes of others without compromising basic Christian principles?
5. In the light of Paul's epistles, is the age of letter-

writing over? What part can it play in Christian service today?

6. Paul was adaptable in his presentation of the Christian Gospel. His visit to Athens was one example of this. What approach do you think he would use today if he spoke to our friends and contemporaries? What would he choose as his starting points?